ENDGAME FOR THE CENTRE LEFT?

About Policy Network

Policy Network is an international thinktank and research institute. Its network spans national borders across Europe and the wider world with the aim of promoting the best progressive thinking on the major social and economic challenges of the 21st century.

Our work is driven by a network of politicians, policymakers, business leaders, public service professionals, and academic researchers who work on long-term issues relating to public policy, political economy, social attitudes, governance and international affairs. This is complemented by the expertise and research excellence of Policy Network's international team.

A platform for research and ideas

- Promoting expert ideas and political analysis on the key economic, social and political challenges of our age.
- Disseminating research excellence and relevant knowledge to a wider public audience through interactive policy networks, including interdisciplinary and scholarly collaboration.
- Engaging and informing the public debate about the future of European and global progressive politics.

A network of leaders, policymakers and thinkers

- Building international policy communities comprising individuals and affiliate institutions.
- Providing meeting platforms where the politically active, and potential leaders of the future, can engage with each other across national borders and with the best thinkers who are sympathetic to their broad aims.
- Engaging in external collaboration with partners including higher education institutions, the private sector, thinktanks, charities, community organisations, and trade unions.
- Delivering an innovative events programme combining in-house seminars with large-scale public conferences designed to influence and contribute to key public debates.

www.policy-network.net

ENDGAME FOR THE CENTRE LEFT?

The Retreat of Social Democracy Across Europe

policy network

ROWMAN &
LITTLEFIELD
——————INTERNATIONAL——————

London • New York

Published by Rowman & Littlefield International Ltd.
Unit A, Whitacre, 26-34 Stannary Street, London, SE11 4AB
www.rowmaninternational.com

Rowman & Littlefield International Ltd. is an affiliate of Rowman & Littlefield
4501 Forbes Boulevard, Suite 200, Lanham, Maryland 20706, USA
With additional offices in Boulder, New York, Toronto (Canada), and Plymouth (UK)
www.rowman.com

British Library Cataloguing in Publication Data
A catalogue record for this book is available from the British Library

ISBN: PB 978-1-78660-282-4
ISBN: eBook 978-1-78660-283-1

Library of Congress Cataloging-in-Publication Data
Library of Congress Control Number: 2016954179

∞ ™ The paper used in this publication meets the minimum requirements
of American National Standard for Information Sciences—Permanence of Paper
for Printed Library Materials, ANSI/NISO Z39.48-1992.

Printed in the United States of America

CONTENTS

ABOUT THE AUTHOR

Patrick Diamond is co-chair and research director at Policy Network. He is a lecturer in Public Policy at Queen Mary, University of London, Gwilym Gibbon fellow at Nuffield College, Oxford, and a visiting fellow in the Department of Politics at the University of Oxford. Until May 2010 he was head of policy planning in 10 Downing Street and senior policy adviser to the prime minister.

PREFACE

This short book is a contribution to the growing debate on the left in
Europe about the future of social democracy, and the likely prospects
for left of centre politics. After a period of electoral dominance,
centre-left parties in western Europe have suffered a dramatic erosion of support; the vote share enjoyed by social democrats is at its
lowest ever level. Already, much has been written about why social
democracy is in a state of decline; political diagnosis is essential
to understand what strategies might now be available to centre-left
parties. This book's argument is that social democracy stands at a
point of great promise, but also peril. To write off centre left politics
now would be a great mistake: right and centre-right competitor parties have their own problems; in any case, societies have not rejected
social democratic values. The ideal of solidarity and the imperative
of forging bonds of connection in a volatile, interdependent world is
as compelling as it always was.

At the same time, the centre left clearly faces difficulties: 'the
forward march of labour' has been abruptly halted while declining
trust in politics adds to the problem of constructing viable electoral
coalitions. The UK's decision to vote to leave the European Union
on June 23 raises the prospect of societies throughout Europe irrepa-
rably divided between voters who embrace economic openness, and

those who are opposed to change. Social democracy has to find new ways to build bridges between 'open' and 'closed' communities by updating public institutions and policies, just as socialist parties did in the immediate aftermath of the second world war. This is an urgent task. There is not a moment to lose.

INTRODUCTION

Over the past decade, social democratic parties across western Europe have been in ignominious retreat. The centre left's electoral decline has been unprecedented. Even where social democrats have attained governmental power, often in coalition with other parties, their experience has been unhappy, followed rapidly by defeat. As a result, many commentators insist that social democracy has lost its vitality, and is destined to wane as a political force and an ideological tradition in Europe. This book considers the factors behind social democracy's decline over the past decade, giving particular attention to the rise of populist counter-movements across the European Union. It then looks ahead at the future of centre-left politics in Europe with an eye towards potential strategies for stemming the left's demise.

The central argument is that for all the difficulties facing social democracy, pessimism can be overstated: despite the apparent demise of centre-left politics, a new progressive era is within reach underpinned by renewed government activism and a new collectivism that goes beyond the traditional state; the new politics of left reform has the potential to fashion a more egalitarian capitalism and a fairer, more inclusive society. This age of progressive reform will be rooted in new electoral coalitions, new governing strategies, and new political narratives.

It is always tempting to search for social trends that might presage a dramatic shift in the centre of gravity towards the left.

However, structural change does not have any pre-determined effect on the fortunes of parties: in the early 20th century, the growth of the working class was supposed to ensure the rise of socialism eclipsing Europe's Conservative and Christian democratic parties. In the aftermath of the second world war, it was feared that the structural decline of the working class and the growth of affluence and mass prosperity would destroy social democracy. But electoral majorities are there to be forged from the raw material of social change; this depends on the skill with which parties develop new ideas and create a language that can appeal to the board majority. The 2008 crisis was heralded as a 'social democratic moment' in the industrialised countries, but the opportunity was squandered as too many centre-left politicians believed that a crisis of the capitalist system would lead inevitably to a rise in support for the left. They failed to cultivate a new generation of progressive ideas and policy programmes akin to the advance of Keynesianism in the 1930s. It is to this vital task that social democrats must now turn.

In Britain, politics on the left has never been more insular or parochial. Within the Labour party, the problems afflicting UK social democracy have been viewed through an almost entirely British lens. Under the present Labour leadership, the belief in 'socialism in one country' has returned with a vengeance. The UK's decision on 23 June to 'leave' the EU is in danger of reinforcing a turn away from the Labour party's historic commitment to internationalism and pro-Europeanism. Yet whether or not Britain remains an EU member, the road to electoral and political recovery for the Labour party will only be found by actively learning from the experience of social democratic parties in other countries across Europe.

THE ELECTORAL LANDSCAPE

Today, social democratic parties and governments are undeniably operating against a backdrop of political uncertainty and electoral volatility: this relates not only to one of the most severe financial crises in the west's history. Capitalism is undergoing major structural alterations: the rate of technological innovation and the decline of industrial-era mass production imply that advanced economies are on the brink of a 'fourth' disruptive industrial revolution, which is undermining existing political and economic institutions. Moreover, fiscal pressures unleashed by the financial crisis are placing unprecedented strain on the public finances, welfare systems and future shape of the state. Crisis 'aftershocks' are accentuating the impact of long-term demographic trends, from an ageing society to declining fertility rates (Sage et al, 2015). The global context is being further reshaped by the rising power of the emerging economies and the relative decline of the west.

The energy and sense of historical purpose that gave birth to social democracy in the late 19th century have faded. Across the industrialised world, the pendulum has swung against the centre left to the surprise of many commentators. The 2008 crisis was predicted to herald a dramatic shift in social democracy's favour, leading to a 'centre-left moment'. The political discourse of advanced capitalist countries has become more concerned with inequality; the disorder wreaked by international finance; the consequences of inadequate regulation in financial markets; and the fragile moral foundations of global capitalism. The great recession has been accompanied by renewed concerns about the impact of technological change and automation on the labour market and the future of employment. Identifying effective remedies for 'capitalist crises' is territory that should naturally aid social democratic parties, as economies struggle to cope with one of the deepest and most painful recessions in 80 years.

Counterintuitively, however, the crisis appears to have benefited the moderate centre right and the populist far right, both of which have adeptly exploited the politics of austerity. The moderate right does this by redefining centre-left parties as profligate and economically incompetent. Those moderate parties are themselves being challenged, however, by the rise of populist parties even further to the right, particularly in northern Europe, that deftly exploit voters' anxieties and insecurities about the increasingly globalised society they inhabit. In last year's Danish elections, for example, it was the rightwing People's party rather than the Conservative moderates that drove former prime minister Helle Thorning-Schmidt's left coalition from power. In Austria, the presidential candidate of the hard right Freedom Party was in touching distance of victory.

The shattering of confidence in global capitalism and the return of state intervention to the centre of political debate has done little to revive support for the left. The 2014 European parliamentary elections could hardly have been worse for the centre left and sent a clear warning signal, resulting in its lowest representation since 1979. In Germany, the SPD has recorded its worst results since the 1890s, despite a very modest improvement in the last federal elections. In Spain, the Spanish Socialist Workers' party (Psoe) has done poorly. The Irish Labour party's vote halved from 14 to 7 per cent. In the Netherlands, the Labour party (PvDA) polled less than 10 per cent. In France, where the left had returned to government, the omens are far from auspicious for next year's presidential elections.

In 2010 and 2015 at the national level, British Labour suffered among its worst defeats since 1918. In Sweden, the 'heartland' of European social democracy, the centre left lost two consecutive parliamentary elections for the first time in over a century, before scraping back to power. Italy provides the only robust evidence for European centre-left optimism. Prime Minister Matteo Renzi's Democratic party obtained more than 40 per cent of the vote in the 2014 elections. However, Italian politics are notoriously volatile while Renzi suffered a recent setback in regional elections, placing the left a long way from building a viable political coalition. The prospect of a centre-left renaissance across Europe is more distant than ever, while the historical achievements of postwar social democracy – universal welfare, high-quality public services, the social investment state – are vulnerable as never before. In electoral terms, social democracy is on the back foot.

Of course, incumbent centre-right parties have fared poorly too. There is arguably a reaction against establishment parties across Europe, as politicians struggle to overcome the long-term legacy of the financial crisis: lower growth, declining living standards, rising inequality and acute fiscal pressures. European centre-left parties' electoral underperformance can be explained by weak and unpopular leadership; lack of a credible alternative, especially on economic management; and the cost of internal divisions in unstable coalition governments. It is not just that social democrats are losing elections, however. In the face of growing economic turmoil and escalating government debt, many now question whether social democracy is even capable of a revival. The centre-left, it is argued, lacks a persuasive electoral and ideological programme and has no credible governing strategy. It is far from impossible that we might be witnessing the slow, painful death of social democracy.

THE STRUCTURAL CAUSES OF DECLINE

These problems are compounded by structural shifts that are eating away at social democratic parties' support base, as economic and social change reshapes the centre left's electoral coalition. And as the structural environment changes, social democratic ideas that were largely accepted in most western European countries in the aftermath of the second world war become increasingly open to challenge. The welfare state's universalism and commitment to addressing unmet material needs has shifted to a focus on enforcing the rules of contribution and responsibility. The perceived legitimacy of centre-left beliefs and values is apparently eroding. It is clear that major social and economic trends are continuing to transform politics.

Two broader historical shifts have challenged social democrats since the end of the cold war. The first is globalisation, characterised not only by worldwide market integration but also by deregulation and liberalisation, which significantly embolden capital at the expense of labour and the state. The second is the structural weakening of democratic politics in comparison to markets and other economic forces, which raises serious questions for a movement such as social democracy, whose existence depends on articulating 'the primacy of politics' in achieving social progress.

Both the liberalisation of global economic activity and the weakening of representative democracy have a crucial impact on centre-left parties. Globalisation has revolutionised economics and politics, with major consequences for traditional institutions but while the global economy has created unprecedented gains in economic growth and living standards, the benefits have not been evenly distributed. Moreover, globalisation no longer seems capable of generating an improved standard of living for those outside the economic and political elite. As a result, there is a strong political backlash against the global economy, expressed most visibly in hostility to liberal migration regimes and to European integration. Cosmopolitanism is now challenged by rising levels of xenophobia, motivated by new insecurities about national identity and belonging. Meanwhile, the institutions of global capitalism are increasingly distrusted following the financial crisis. This was the backdrop to the UK's decision to 'leave' the EU in June 2016.

In the meantime, just as globalisation and liberalisation place new strains on the social and economic fabric of western states, political institutions appear less capable of dealing with these adversities. A '24-hour media' cycle and the scrutiny of social media have made politics more transparent, but also more vulnerable to attack. The public mistrust of politicians and political institutions has weakened their legitimacy, as evidenced in lower turnouts at national elections. Voters demand quick results, even though achieving political change is as arduous as ever: the German sociologist, Max Weber, famously described the exercise of democratic politics as "the strong and slow boring of hard boards". Moreover, confidence in EU institutions has never been weaker. As governments confront increasingly global challenges, they lack transnational mechanisms that can deal with interdependence while ensuring democratic legitimacy and consent (Gamble, 2010).

The decline of social democratic politics, combined with the rise of globalisation and the weakening of representative democracy, have long-term implications for the future of social democracy throughout Europe, as well as for Europe's political left.

THE CURRENT WEAKNESS OF THE SOCIAL DEMOCRATIC IDEA

What, then, are the structural weaknesses that underlie the perfor-mance of social democratic parties? Shortly before the millennium, the late sociologist Ralf Dahrendorf famously wrote of the "end of the social democratic century". For him, the third way and other 'revisionist' projects were largely fruitless efforts by the left to remain relevant in a transformed political landscape. Darendorf's view resonates with those who believe that social democracy's mission had already been accomplished, given that today's centre-left programmes form part of any 'mainstream' political menu. Hence, there is no longer anything specific or challenging about social democracy; the programmes of centre-left parties offer no impending threat to the status quo, nor do they promise to protect working-class interests against the forces of international capitalism.

A less benign reading might conclude that social democracy has been fighting a losing battle since the process of globalisation has-tened by the end of the cold war. The period after the second world war saw the emergence of a model of nation state social democracy in which national solidarity trumped international class consciousness. It was a period defined by the aim of improving the material condi-tions of the working class within fixed national boundaries, primarily through the use of redistribution and social security (Berman, 2006). But with greater global and European integration following the cold war, spurred on by the rise of international economic competition as well as migration, a 'defensive' mindset increasingly dominated thinking on the left. Centre-left parties became conservative, deter-mined merely to defend the gains of the postwar period.

On top of this, the new wave of globalisation and market capital-ism weakened collectivist institutions, promoting an increasingly individualistic society while eroding class identity and solidar-ity. In effect, the end of the cold war marked the demise of any ambitious social democratic vision, even if it enabled the centre left to separate itself from the excesses of state socialism. As the significance of class faded, social cleavages formed around migration and identity, spawned new populist movements on the left and right.

MIGRATION, INTEGRATION AND IDENTITY

Social and demographic change poses major questions about the future sustainability and structure of the European welfare state; concerns have mounted over migration's social impact across the EU, despite the economic and cultural benefits that migrants bring to member states. The success of the far right and its anti-immigration agenda in the 2014 European parliamentary elections, as well as in the recent Brexit campaign, is testament to social democracy's decline.

The widening gap between rich and poor within the EU has ensured migration becomes a major political issue. Rising levels of unemployment in the aftermath of the great recession inevitably influenced attitudes toward European immigration. As the economic crisis recedes, the 'new' Europe is experiencing important and, in some instances, troubling political developments and social tensions. The EU's expansion to the east combined with southern Europe's economic stagnation has emboldened new political forces that threaten the mainstream political system.

This was on display in recent elections, as countries across Europe witnessed the rise to prominence of so-called populist parties. Though some parties came from the left, such as Syriza and Podemos, others are harder to classify, like Italy's Five Star Movement. Nonetheless, the vast majority of electoral gains made by populists came from the right. In three major western European countries in the European elections – Denmark, the UK and France – rightwing populists topped the poll.

Many of these parties, including those on the left, derive their support from those citizens who are deeply alienated from the EU. This disaffection is a product of the EU's apparent lack of democratic accountability, encouragement of the uncontrolled free movement of labour, and the imposition of austerity. Indeed, austerity has driven support for both the populist left and right; in the south, voters have leaned toward parties determined to scale back austerity, while many in the north feel they have already paid the price for southern 'profligacy'.

With the notable exception of Greece and Spain, however, the left in the EU has failed to capitalise on the crisis as the right has done. The performance of green parties exemplifies this trend. The only country where green parties have been successful was in Portugal, where the Democratic Unitarian Coalition and the Earth party won a combined share of the vote of nearly 20 per cent. This fits with the broader pattern of the growth of the radical left in Europe's south. The wider picture of green performance in Europe is one of stagnation. Most countries have seen no change in the number of green members of parliament.

More importantly, the rise of radical and populist parties is fracturing support for traditional social democratic parties. The growth of the populists is challenging the hegemony that centre-left parties have enjoyed in Europe since the second world war. Although there are more 'right-leaning' governments in Europe than 'left-leaning' ones, centrist political parties are increasingly forced to work together in coalition governments. Only two EU states currently have one-party centre-left majorities: Malta and Slovakia. Though once considered temporary and the by-product of electoral arithmetic, coalitions that span the two wings of the centre are increasingly seen as the norm. In the future, they might be fundamental to holding back the populist tide, but the danger is that establishment parties become vulnerable to populist forces who exploit the unpopularity that inevitably follows incumbency.

The European political landscape has transformed dramatically since the financial crisis. In northern countries, many social democratic voters – disillusioned with the EU, immigration and fiscal bailouts for the south – have shifted their support to parties of the populist right. Mistrust in political institutions and dissatisfaction with democracy have hardened these divisions. Southern Europeans are now far more sceptical than those in the north toward both the EU and their national governments, cultivating support for anti-establishment movements like Podemos and Syriza. This is accompanied by a shift in the ideological character of politics in the north and south: where the gravity of political debate in the north has often moved rightwards, in the south it has shifted left, making it harder for social democratic parties to survive in an electoral environment where the centre is declining at the expense of the extremes (Sage et al, 2015).

WHAT NEXT FOR EUROPEAN SOCIAL DEMOCRACY?

Europe's social democrats are facing an increasingly pessimistic future in the face of repeated electoral defeats; but they should not lose hope. After all, the world still needs the values and programmes that centre-left parties espouse. So what should the priorities be for reviving social democracy? Intellectually, there are two major challenges ahead relating to the politics of economic competence, and the politics of identity. In the 1990s, third way centre-left governments undermined themselves by becoming too close to market liberalism. In the wake of the Berlin Wall's collapse, they came to the inevitable conclusion that western capitalism had triumphed: to gain office, social democratic parties had to run a market economy at least as efficiently as the right. But the result was ideological capitulation. Many of the policy regimes and institutions developed in the immediate aftermath of the second world war were swiftly abandoned.

This was not wholly misguided. Left parties did need to demonstrate they could manage the capitalist economy effectively by coming to terms with markets. Moreover, in a globalised economy, prescriptions arising from an earlier application of Keynesian theory had to be revised. We have learned that public spending on the demand side is not all that matters and governments have to attend to supply-side reforms; moreover, the state has to be aware of the impact of fiscal policies on innovation and growth (Aghion, 2014). The problem was that by the time the financial crisis struck in 2008–9, the centre-left appeared complicit in the policy decisions that led to the crash. In particular, social democrats had largely given up effective regulation and supervision of the financial sector, alongside any wider objective of strategic intervention to rebalance the economy. The left today needs to rethink its economic approach in order to create a fairer, more resilient and sustainable capitalism, while rejecting the claim that governments have no business intervening in markets. This willingness to intervene is all the more necessary given the 'existential' threat posed by climate change: the 2015 Paris agreement was an important step forward, but with global growth of three per cent per annum following two centuries of rapid industrialisation, new ways must be found to deal with the potentially devastating impact of environmental pressures.[1]

The second task relates to the politics of identity. Across western Europe, social democratic parties have been damaged by the insinuation that they are no longer committed to defending national interests and borders. The centre left needs to demonstrate that there is no contradiction between a commitment to national interests – to patriotism and pride in the nation state – alongside the need for a stronger Europe. Only by working together can EU countries address common security and economic challenges while also defending their national interests. At the same time, national electorates will only accept the case for international cooperation if they feel confident in their own national identity. The overwhelmingly liberal, cosmopolitan values that prevail among the progressive left have to be balanced by the recognition that national solidarity and shared values matter to our citizens. They should start by being prepared to revisit fundamental principles such as 'freedom of movement' in Europe in order to address voters' concerns about political and economic dislocation; this theme is considered further in the concluding chapter.

But social democracy needs more than ideas if it is to flourish in the future; it needs political organisation. Centre-left politics must continue to be anchored in citizen mobilisation rather than ignoring the politics of protest and dissent. Social democratic parties have always drawn strength from practical activism and bottom-up campaigning. Left parties must remain insurgents even when they are in government, refusing to become part of the status quo and continuing to offer solutions to new social challenges and injustices. They must govern responsibly without abandoning the quest for solidarity and equality, embracing a participatory democracy that empowers citizen decision-making. They must continue to recognise 'the primacy of politics' in a changing society: social democracy has a duty to continue to reform political institutions. This is vitally important in western Europe, where representative democracy has been in decline in recent decades.

Social democracy in Europe is not destined to retreat in the years ahead. The electoral setbacks it has suffered since the 1990s have been serious, and the long-term deterioration in social democratic parties' vote share is sobering. The structural obstacles to social democratic reform, such as redistribution and efforts to strengthen welfare states, remain formidable where public attitudes have become harsher and more punitive in recent decades. To overcome these challenges, centre-left parties must make their case more skillfully, framing an appeal relevant to the broad majority of citizens: both those who embrace economic change, and those who increasingly fear openess. Social democrats can draw on a wealth of arguments in remaking centre-left politics, articulating the case for fairness and equality through the vision of an inclusive social and economic future. Making the plight of society's least privileged resonate with the relatively well-off has always been vital for centre-left politics. It is even more so today, given the 'new hard times' that Europe is living through.

NOTE

1. http://speri.dept.shef.ac.uk/2016/07/13/the-coming-crisis-we-do-not-have-much-time/.

THE POLITICAL LANDSCAPE
OF EUROPE

Since the financial crisis in 2008–9, centre-left parties have been performing poorly in almost every EU member state. The present electoral map is bleak; as Figure 1.1 of EU15 countries since 1946 demonstrates, the electoral position of centre-left parties has been in dramatic decline since the late 2000s having risen fairly consistently throughout the postwar years.

The period of electoral decline seems, nonetheless, to have preceded the financial crisis; since the early 1970s, social democracy has undergone a period of 'significant electoral retreat' which worsened during the 2000s.[1] Although the vote share of centre-left parties had

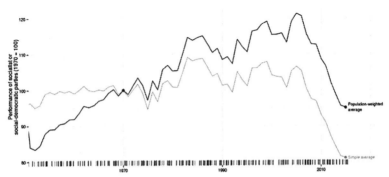

Figure 1.1   The Performance of Social Democratic Parties in Western Europe[2]

Table 1.2 Electoral Performance of Socialist Parties in Western Europe (Legislative Elections)

	1960–73	1974–79	1980–89	1990–99	2000–07	Most recent election
Austria	46.3	48.1	44.6	37.3	35.9	26.8
Denmark	38.7	32.7	32.2	36.0	26.8	26.3
Norway	42.9	38.6	37.4	36.0	28.5	35.4
Sweden	46.8	43.3	44.5	39.8	37.5	32.1
Germany	41.0	40.2	37.9	36.9	36.4	23.0
UK	45.1	33.6	29.2	38.8	38.0	30.4
Belgium	30.0	27.2	28.2	23.2	24.5	31.4
Netherlands	25.9	31.5	31.0	26.5	21.2	24.8
Finland	24.0	24.9	25.4	24.4	24.4	19.1
Spain	—	39.3	44.0	38.0	38.4	22.0
Greece	—	34.4	42.2	42.3	40.8	6.3
Portugal	—	28.9	27.2	39.1	41.5	32.3
France	16.8	32.1	34.7	20.7	24.4	28.6

Based on data in G. Moschonas, 'Electoral Dynamics and Social Democratic Identity: Socialism and its changing constituencies in France, Great Britain, Sweden and Denmark'.

eroded, many experts resisted the claim that social democracy was in a state of terminal decline: after all, centre-left parties in most countries were one of two dominant political formations and therefore likely to gain support to form a government at some point in the near future (Moschonas, 2008). More recent trends indicate this may be rather optimistic: even in the UK, where the Labour party's position is entrenched by the first-past-the-post electoral system, there are indications that the traditional two-party system is gradually breaking down.

In recent years, social democrats in western Europe have either been in government, where they have experienced record unpopularity such as in France, or they have been weak junior members of coalition governments with limited room for political manoeuvre, such as Germany and the Netherlands. The French socialists have been divided since François Hollande's presidential victory in 2011: the traditional left in the party sought to put forward a radical alternative to austerity based on higher personal and corporate taxation, while the reformists now backed by President Hollande battled to reform

France's apparently arcane labour regulations and introduce tighter controls on public spending.[3] This is a reaction to the deep structural problems afflicting the French economy; nonetheless, Hollande is the most unpopular president in France since polling began.[4]

In the Netherlands, the PvDA has had to cope with much greater electoral volatility as the result of new economic and cultural cleavages over immigration and European integration.[5] As a member of the coalition government, the PvDA has acceded to a major austerity programme including cuts in provision for the elderly which has alienated its core supporters, having promised previously to return to traditional social democracy.[6] In Germany, the SPD entered another 'grand coalition' with Merkel's Christian Democrats in 2013; the dilemma for the SPD is how to differentiate its approach in a coalition, especially when the refugee crisis has antagonised its own working-class supporters. In fairness, according to the Economist "the SPD extracted some big concessions as a price for entering the coalition", notably the minimum wage and capping rents in German cities.[7] Nonetheless, the French Socialists and the German SPD have not succeeded in forging a shared approach to the eurozone crisis and austerity: in Germany, fiscal conservatism still prevails, even on the left, and the momentum for shifting the policy approach towards a 'European growth compact' has stalled.

Scandinavia has traditionally been the heartland of European social democracy, but even here, the omens for the centre left are hardly propitious. In Sweden, Stefan Löfven's Social Democrats failed to secure an overall majority in national elections despite an unpopular centre-right government. The Social Democrats had already declined dramatically in the polls before the eruption of the refugee crisis; they came to power apparently lacking a political project for Sweden's future. The consensus among Swedish voters in favour of immigration appears to be collapsing amid rising support in the polls for the Sweden Democrats.[8] In the meantime, in Denmark the Social Democrats were ejected from government in 2015, despite becoming the largest party amid rising support for the populist right. The resignation of Helle Thorning-Schmidt as leader led to the installation of Mette Frederiksen who has vowed to continue with the policies of 'economic responsibility'; she has signalled an intention to vigorously pursue the interests of 'wage-earners' while affirming the goal of full employment.[9] The Social Democrats have also maintained a tough stance on the recent refugee crisis, refusing to be outflanked by the centre right on policy and rhetoric.[10]

Elsewhere in northern Europe, the British Labour party has suffered two consecutive general election defeats since 2010. The party recovered some support in 2015 achieving 30.4 per cent of the vote, but it won fewer seats due to the catastrophic meltdown of its electoral position in Scotland and its poor performance throughout much of England. Labour's new leader, Jeremy Corbyn, hails from the far left and promises to rejuvenate the party by returning to traditional socialist principles; the polls so far indicate that he is struggling to convince a sceptical electorate despite the fact the governing Conservative party is badly divided over Europe. In Ireland, the Irish Labour party achieved its worst ever result in recent elections having been a junior coalition partner in a 'pro-austerity' coalition government; it won only seven parliamentary seats compared to 33 at the previous election. Nonetheless, there is speculation that the party might return to government, although many believe Labour must now go into opposition and rebuild its position from the backbenches.[11]

The socialist parties of southern Europe, notably Greece and Spain, have demonstrated growing strength since the 1980s, but they have been eclipsed since the financial crash. In Greece, the social democratic party, Pasok, sought to present itself as a force for national stability, but was catastrophically divided when the former prime minister, George Papandreou, formed a breakaway party, Kidiso (the Movement of Democrats and Socialists).[12] This led to a splintering of votes on the centre left towards the radical alternative, Syriza; in the most recent Greek elections, Pasok achieved only 6.3 per cent of the popular vote. Syriza has moderated its position by doing what is necessary to keep Greece within the eurozone, further squeezing Pasok on the centre left. Syriza's leader, Alexis Tsipras, has been able to execute this 'U-turn' since the majority of his voters want to moderate austerity, rather than leave the euro.[13] This has left Pasok electorally and politically bereft. In Spain, Psoe achieved its worst ever result in the December 2015 elections, securing 90 parliamentary seats and 22 per cent of the vote. While Psoe was pivotal to the coalition negotiations, since a majority of votes went to parties of the left, the options did not appear palatable and there were fresh elections in June 2016. The PP secured 137 seats while Psoe managed to hold on to second place against a strong challenge from the left-populist party, Podemos, which secured 85 seats and 22.7 per cent of the vote.[14] However, the problem for the Psoe is that any agreement with Podemos might rupture the Psoe's own internal organisation, particularly over the issue of the future of Catalonia; a national unity government with Mariano Rajoy's PP would be popular with the European Union and the financial sector, but it would simply reinforce the perception that the mainstream parties in Spain are 'all the same'.[15] The risk would be a further haemorrhage of votes away from Psoe. In Portugal meanwhile, the Social Democrats have entered a fragile coalition with other 'leftist' parties.

The exception to the rule of centre-left gloom in southern Europe is, of course, Italy. Matteo Renzi's government has had some success in pursuing structural reforms to reduce taxes on employment and property boosting the private sector, aided by improvements in the performance of the Italian economy; according to the finance minister, Pier Carlo Padoan, "Italy is back".[16] The question for Renzi's government is whether further progress can be made in reforming the Italian constitution and taking additional steps to prevent corruption; the prime minister faces a difficult referendum on constitutional reform later this year which he might well lose. Similarly, Malta has a successful centre-left administration in place.

The collapse of social democracy in eastern and central Europe since the 1990s has been remarkable. Astonishingly, Poland currently has no mainstream left parliamentary representation, as the

Left Coalition failed to gain enough votes to beat the 8 per cent threshold, while the post-Communist SLD appear in danger of becoming obsolete.[17] The Polish left has completely fragmented with an array of parties jostling for position and influence. The Czech Republic is currently governed by a social democratic prime minister, but elsewhere in the accession countries, Conservative parties prevail; even Hungary has shifted towards authoritarianism.[18]

Centre-left parties are not in government because they are losing elections; they are defeated predominantly because their electorates are fragmenting towards 'challenger' parties on the left and the right. The causes of defeat vary between countries: having decried capitalism since the financial crisis, social democratic parties seem more interested in debating problems than proposing concrete solutions; and on the major challenges of migration, security and terrorism confronting Europe, social democrats appear to have little new or important to say.[19] Social democracy is not only electorally moribund; it lacks a 'big idea' for the future of European society. Against this backdrop, it seems plausible to predict the demise of the mainstream social democratic left in Europe. The chapter that follows will address which key voter groups the left is losing.

NOTES

1. G. Moschonas, 'Electoral Dynamics and Social Democratic Identity: Socialism and its changing constituencies in France, Great Britain, Sweden and Denmark', What's Left of the Left: Liberalism and Social Democracy in a Globalised World, A Working Conference, Centre for European Studies, Harvard University, May 9–10th, 2008.

2. https://medium.com/@chrishanretty/electorally-west-european-social-democrats-are-at-their-lowest-point-for-forty-years-ac7ae3d8ddb7#.degh68hxd

3. http://www.reuters.com/article/us-france-socialists-insight-idUSKBN0IG0H520141027

4. http://www.politico.eu/article/long-goodbye-of-the-european-left-francois-hollande/

5. http://library.fes.de/pdf-files/id/ipa/07953.pdf

6. http://www.policy-network.net/pno_detail.aspx?ID=4604

7. http://www.economist.com/news/europe/21601312-indulging-her-social-democratic-coalition-partners-angela-merkel-risks-turning-germany

8. http://www.policy-network.net/pno_detail.aspx?ID=4973&title=The-summer-Sweden-became-obsessed-with-immigration

9. http://www.policy-network.net/pno_detail.aspx?ID=4972&title=Frederiksens-balancing-act

10. http://www.policy-network.net/pno_detail.aspx?ID=5046&title=Denmarks-centre-left-is-in-disarray-over-the-refugee-crisis

11. http://www.dailymail.co.uk/wires/reuters/article-3543275/Irelands-Labour-Party-considering-entering-government.html

12. http://www.policy-network.net/pno_detail.aspx?ID=4834&title=Greeces-shifting-political-landscape.

13. http://www.policy-network.net/pno_detail.aspx?ID=4979&title=How-did-Syriza-manage-to-win-in-spite-of-its-U-turn

14. https://www.theguardian.com/world/2016/jun/27/spanish-elections-mariano-rajoy-to-build-coalition-peoples-party

15. http://www.policy-network.net/pno_detail.aspx?ID=5049&title=Que-ser%C3%A1-ser%C3%A1-%E2%80%A6-whatever-will-be

16. http://www.policy-network.net/pno_detail.aspx?ID=5013&title=Italy-is-back-%E2%80%93-but-so-are-Renzis-PD-pains

17. http://www.policy-network.net/pno_detail.aspx?ID=5011&title=Where-now-for-the-Polish-left

18. http://www.politico.eu/article/long-goodbye-of-the-european-left-francois-hollande/

19. http://www.politico.eu/article/long-goodbye-of-the-european-left-francois-hollande/

WHICH VOTERS ARE
THE LEFT LOSING?

This chapter examines how the long-term erosion of support for social democratic parties among voters can be explained. The prevailing view among political scientists is that having repositioned themselves in the centre ground as 'catch-all' parties after the second world war, social democrats have alienated their traditional working-class supporters, just as they have gained a new, but precarious, base of middle-class support. New Labour in the UK is an exemplar of the shift, but the German SPD and the Swedish Social Democratic party are both held to have moved in a similar modernising 'neoliberal' direction.

There is support for the claim that becoming 'catch-all' parties with moderated policy positions does have adverse electoral consequences for social democrats. It appears that in most countries, working-class voters have defected from centre-left parties towards the radical left and more often, the populist right; whereas social democratic parties were once part of the process of 'democratic class struggle' and decommodification through the development of the welfare state, they no longer perform that historical role.[1] This argument nonetheless underplays the structural impact of class de-alignment alongside disenchantment with established political movements on the decline in support for the left. Such a perspective implies that if only centre-left parties embraced statist social democracy, all would be well. The focus on the 'traditional working class' ignores structural change and misunderstands how economic insecurity has spread to new occupational groups in society. Middle-class support for social democracy has grown among the 'salaried middle strata' and the 'educated and intellectual professions'.[2] The primary reason why social democratic parties appear to be losing elections, however, is that the support base of social democracy has fragmented over the last three decades.

FRAGMENTATION AS 'THE NEW NORMAL'

Centre-left parties are confronting a political dilemma that is far from new: their coalition of support is fracturing as the secular decline of the manual working class has forced them to seek middle-class votes which do not solidify into enduring electoral coalitions. This is a political environment characterised by a breakdown in 'hereditary voting patterns' and the erosion of stable political affiliations (Moschonas, 2008). In the main, electorates are more fragmented and volatile than in the 'golden age' of postwar social democracy. Social democratic parties are operating in a world of 'relative class-lessness' characterised by 'a diverse and fluid electorate in which socially structured partisanship is weak, while the potential for volatility is high and increasing' (Padgett, 2003: 47). Moreover, unprecedented numbers of voters no longer participate in the political system. John Callaghan (2009) emphasises that social democracy has been increasingly under pressure, as the case for the traditional activist state has been undermined. From the right, neoliberalism has emphasised the negation of the state in favour of the market; from the left, the culture of 'left libertarianism' has further challenged statism and collectivism (Callaghan, 2009). The goal of centre-left parties is to forge enduring political coalitions in a more segmented and fractured political environment. The emphasis, as ever, is on reconciling seemingly divergent, if not contradictory strategic interests.

CULTURE AND CLASS

Much previous analysis has adopted the more traditional lens of analysing social democracy's electoral coalition in terms of voter groups centred on a broad notion of social class. Yet across western societies, the relationship between class identity and partisan affiliation has substantially broken down: culture is increasingly seen to trump economics. An alternative framework involves understanding voter groups in terms of cultural 'types' rather than occupational categories. This is more sophisticated than the dualism which is frequently posited in the literature between 'communitarian' and 'cosmopolitan' voters (Callaghan, 2009). In Callaghan's schema, for example:

- *Traditionalist voters* emphasise material solidarity, traditional forms of collectivism, the preservation of postwar welfare states, alongside the importance of class-based social movements such as the trade unions. They are often resistant to developments in the European Union, for example greater freedom of movement and labour mobility.
- *Modernist voters* place a high premium on individual achievement and aspiration alongside material economic growth and improvements in living standards. They are broadly sympathetic to the 'consumerist' agenda of politics putting an emphasis on material prosperity. They are wary of growing government spending and any rise in the overall tax burden.
- *Post-materialist voters* prioritise quality of life, emphasising ecological concerns, the climate change transition, and environmental sustainability as key political imperatives. They are often relatively 'cash rich' but 'time poor', valuing greater freedom from paid work.
- *Hedonistic 'post-modernist' voters* are libertarian 'pleasure-seekers' who stress the importance of freedom and civil liberties. They are generally 'anti-statist' and particularly drawn towards the potential of new technology as well as markets. They are

enemies of paternalism and want greater autonomy to govern their own lives (Callaghan, 2009:47).

What is apparent from Callaghan's approach is the difficulty of constructing a political coalition across these social groups given the apparently sharp divergence in social and political attitudes and interests. Nick Lowles and Anthony Painter (2011) have similarly developed this sociological typology analysing the 'new tribes of identity politics' drawing largely on empirical data from the UK:

- Their first group are *confident multiculturals* predominantly drawn from the professional and managerial occupational classes. They have a tendency to support centre-left and green parties, and are generally positive about diversity, cosmopolitanism, and mass immigration, believing that western societies do well from globalisation.
- Second, *mainstream liberals* who have similar values to multi-culturals and are also well-educated. They may be more scepti-cal about immigration but still regard it as a 'net benefit' to their country.
- Third, *identity ambivalents* do not have this degree of confi-dence in the future, and are generally less optimistic about their country's potential. They tend to be ambivalent about immigration given its impact on public services and social housing on which they are often dependent. This group often includes black and minority ethnic voters.
- Fourth, *culturally integrationist* voters are in the main older and more prosperous, tending to support centre-right Conservative parties. According to Lowles and Painter, this group's concern about immigration relates to national identity and integration, rather than pressure on living standards and public services.
- Fifth, *latent hostiles* are less well-educated, and fearful of the impact of immigration and globalisation on their economic prospects and way of life. They want political parties to defend national identity and the distinctive values of their societies.

- The final group exhibit *active enmity*: they display open hostility to immigrants and are generally intolerant of religious and ethnic differences. These voters are the most disengaged from the formal political system and are often prepared to support far-right parties.

According to Lowles and Painter's data, around 25 per cent of the sampled population are essentially cosmopolitan liberals ('confident multiculturals' and 'mainstream liberals'). Approximately 50 per cent are broadly ambivalent, some because of economics, others because of cultural factors ('identity ambivalents' and 'culturally integrationists'). A further 25 per cent are actively hostile to immigration and multiculturalism ('latent hostiles' and the 'active enmity' group). Lowles and Painter map their identity categories onto social class too, but find the relationship is rarely determinate. For instance, a small proportion of 'confident multiculturals' are drawn from the lowest socioeconomic class; the highest socioeconomic group is strongly represented within the 'cultural integrationist' category. This finding demonstrates the inadequacy of the 'cosmopolitan/communitarian' dichotomy in understanding the prospects for social democratic politics. A significant challenge for social democracy is the tendency for a high proportion of centre-left support to come from 'identity ambivalents', despite the generally multiculturalist orientation of centre-left parties in western Europe. This explains the volatility that often characterises the performance of social democratic parties.

The 'traditional working class' which is still seen as the natural 'heartland' of European social democratic parties is declining relative to the size of the population. One recent study of social class argued that 'new social formations appear to be emerging out of the tendrils of the traditional working class'. According to the thinktank Demos: 'As the pre-war cohort shrinks as a proportion of the population, therefore, we can expect the balance of opinion in the population as a whole to move in a more liberal direction'. Today's 'working class' is actually comprised of a diversity of suburban voters, graduates, young people, service workers, and so on (*The Economist*, 'The new working class', 16th June 2014). The 'new working class' is better-educated and more diverse, but also increasingly aware of economic insecurity which is spreading to those in traditionally middle-class occupations where there are few links to the labour and trade union movement.

This point is emphasised by Anne Wren (2013) who notes that there has been a major shift in the type of workers exposed to international competition. Whereas in the 1970s and 1980s 'blue-collar' workers in less skilled occupations were particularly vulnerable to global competitive pressures, today middle-class professionals find themselves under growing threat. The ICT revolution has meant that high-skilled employment in service sectors such as finance, the law, media and business has become more internationally traded, increasing middle-class exposure to global competition and heightening job insecurity (Wren, 2013). This is attenuated by the impact of new technologies and automation across the labour force; European social democratic parties have to respond to 'the international rise of the new working class'. Wren (2013) concludes that highly skilled workers in sectors that are more exposed to global competition may be less sympathetic to spending on redistribution and the welfare state, and are less likely to support centre-left parties. There are progressively fewer middle-class professionals in 'sheltered' public sector occupations prepared to support welfare spending than was the case in the 'golden age' of the post-1945 welfare state (Esping-Andersen, 2009).

CULTURAL IDENTITY AND GENERATIONAL CHANGE

The traditional white working class that has remained, at least symbolically, important to social democratic parties has been in secular decline. The new frontiers of politics are perceived to be about younger generational cohorts: more tolerant, cosmopolitan, outward-looking, and accepting of globalisation, but also more self-reliant and less willing to tolerate poor quality public services.

The 5–75–20 society

Progressive politics stands at a crossroads. On the one hand, the strategic opportunities for social democracy in Europe and the industrialised countries appear propitious. Structural trends in our societies are accentuating inequality, polarisation, social division and insecurity; in the aftermath of the financial crisis, many on the left believe 'the state is back'. On the other hand, weaker lifechances, lack of opportunity and burgeoning insecurity are not only afflicting the traditionally excluded groups. This 'disease' is spreading to the broader middle-class suffering from declining real wages and incomes; these groups are increasingly anxious about the future of employment in the light of global outsourcing, the spread of new technology, and the rise of automation; they are struggling to reconcile the pressures of 'earning' and 'caring' in family life, both for the very young and the very old; and they fear their children's life opportunities will be weaker than those of their parents in the face of rapidly rising asset prices (especially housing), the increasing cost of higher education, and fears about future employment in the light of global competitive challenges. Moreover, the 'new middle class' is as sceptical of 'big' government as it is of global market forces. As such, social democrats need to fashion an inclusive, broad-based strategy that appeals both to those already in the middle class, and those who aspire to get there.

THE NEW INSECURE: TODAY'S MIDDLE CLASS AND THOSE LEFT BEHIND

Every industrialised country will have marked variations in its class structure. Nonetheless, the dominant trend in the last two decades has been towards the development of a '5–75–20' society in the developed economies:

- Roughly five per cent enjoy 'runaway' rewards at the top, as asset prices and returns to wealth soar, a group largely comprised of professionals working in finance and those who have inherited wealth (Bell & Machin, 2014). They are increasingly footloose and globally connected. This group are often criticised for their efforts to evade tax, but they already contribute a growing share of tax revenues.

- The 75 per cent in the middle are either in work or have a retirement income but are relatively insecure; they are anxious about the future. They are not only 'blue-collar' industrial workers threatened by outsourcing, but middle-class professionals who fear their jobs will be next as the emerging 'Mint' economies move quickly up the economic value-chain (Wren, 2013).

- The 20 per cent at the 'bottom' of society are marginalised from the labour market and excluded from most of life's opportunities (Taylor-Gooby, 2013). This group are often dependent on state benefits throughout their lives; their children are at significant risk of poverty.

The issue for social democracy is that historically it has been most concerned with the state of the wealthy and the very poor. The centre left wants to ensure that the rich pay their fair share of tax and that the capitalists behave responsibly. And quite understandably, social democrats want to improve the life chances of the poorest in society. The current focus on inequality since 2008 has accentuated this intellectual orientation even further. Yet it is among the 'anxious middle' that elections are won and lost. As recent studies by Mike Savage and Fiona Devine (2015) demonstrate, relatively few people can be straightforwardly categorised as 'middle-class' or 'working-class'; this is a major challenge to the traditional mindset of social democratic parties.

KEY TRENDS: AUTOMATION, THE 'UNFINISHED' GENDER REVOLUTION, AND THE AGEING SOCIETY

The inequality, polarisation and growing insecurity which characterises the new class structure of the industrialised countries is being exacerbated by structural forces alongside economic and social change. Part of this is evidently to do with new economic forces: technology and automation; globalisation and trade liberalisation; and taxation policies in particular. The starting point is that more than 75 per cent of employment in the OECD countries is now in services (Wren, 2013) and job growth is predominantly occurring in service-orientated sectors (both high- and middle-skill levels).

However, it is the shift in the nature of the service-driven economy which is significant. The analysis of the impact of 'automation' where relatively highly skilled, 'human-capital rich' jobs once performed by people are now performed by machines is increasingly in vogue (Frey & Osbourne, 2013). Technological change not only threatens the position of lower-skilled workers, but those in 'white-collar' and professional occupations. The tendency is for labour productivity gains to increasingly benefit an ever-smaller group at the top, leading to a further squeeze on nominal wages (Irvin, 2014). Moreover, an increasing share of GDP is flowing to capital at the expense of labour as technology replaces human workers. Nonetheless, technological change alone cannot be blamed for rising inequality and adverse economic outcomes.

The increasing volume of trade in the global economy as product, capital and labour markets are more liberalised puts further downward pressure on the wages and incomes of the middle. In many countries (although not the Nordic states), the structures of collective pay bargaining that have traditionally protected middle-class jobs and living standards are being eroded; neither is the public sector a 'safe haven'; the impact of austerity means that insecurity is spreading to the public sector professions (Wren, 2013). As the emerging market economies move up the productivity value-chain, so the competitive threat to workers in the industrialised states grows more acute.

As a result, wage inequalities are accelerating as there is a secular decline in the relative economic position of middle-class households. According to George Irvin (2014) median household incomes in Germany, for example, between 2000 and 2010 have consistently lagged behind GDP growth; in Japan, median incomes have fallen by an average of one per cent a year since 1995; in the UK, median income growth since the mid-2000s has declined to zero. This change in the distribution of growth away from the middle is apparently a structural shift rather than a temporary cyclical trend.

As the impact of these developments has worsened in many industrialised states, taxation systems appear to be becoming less redistributive and progressive. It is sometimes forgotten that postwar taxation and welfare state regimes in northern Europe were widely supported by middle-class groups, not only the poor, recognising that collective social provision and progressivity in the tax base protected their relative position in the distribution of earnings and rewards. Too often, these institutions and systems have been gradually eroded by the growing pressures towards restructuring, targeting and the residualisation of the welfare state: the middle class is losing its stake in social security. Yet the middle '75 per cent' are the new 'cling on' middle class who need collectivised social security to be assured of dignity and income adequacy, especially in retirement (Bell & Machin, 2014).

Nevertheless, there are wider structural trends beyond economic forces that are reshaping the income distribution: one set of social trends relates to what Gosta Esping-Andersen (2009) has termed the 'unfinished' gender revolution in western societies. While the balance of caring and earning roles is being renegotiated between women and men, women continue to face major pay penalties and inequalities in labour market outcomes. Moreover, families are under pressure as the increase in working hours coincides with rising care costs, both for childcare and elderly care. Apart from impacting negatively on family life, the risk is that women particularly are either forced out of employment, or compelled to accept jobs way below their labour market potential, which undermines economic growth and productivity. The 'new' social risks include intergenerational imbalances and gender-related inequalities.

Another set of structural changes in the industrialised countries alludes to the ageing society and demographic change. This is putting growing pressure on welfare systems while potentially weakening long-term growth, as larger numbers of older workers drop out of the labour market. The International Monetary Fund (IMF) recently warned that the impact of demography on the public finances would be considerably greater than the financial crisis: in the EU, the cost of pensions is expected to rise from 10.2 to 12.6 per cent of GDP by 2060; healthcare will increase from 6.7 to 8.2 per cent. Maintaining an active workforce relative to the retired population is necessary in the long term to pay for state services, which is likely to refocus debate about the importance of migration in continental Europe. Europe's high rate of unemployment, particularly youth unemployment, has weakened the long-term viability of welfare states, acting as a drag on growth.

NO RETURN TO 'DEFENSIVE' SOCIAL DEMOCRACY

In the midst of these structural changes, there are undoubtedly opportunities for social democracy to rebuild its political base. What the centre left cannot do, however, is return to what the late Tony Judt termed a doctrine of 'defensive' social democracy. The traditional welfare states of the postwar era cannot be recreated in a world of greater complexity and social change: today's younger generation is a 'networked generation' who identify their interests with flat, non-hierarchical structures, rather than the vertical institutions of the 1945 settlement (Mulgan, 2005). A knee-jerk shift to what Philippe Aghion calls 'bazar Keynesianism' is untenable given the fiscal pressures on the state, and the lack of confidence in conventional Keynesian prescriptions.

Moreover, social democracy will neither find salvation in crude distributional politics, nor the flirtation with political populism. The politics of handing out 'sweeteners' to deserving electoral groups is implausible in an age of acute fiscal constraint, while elevating short-term political tactics above long-term policy is unlikely to produce sustained governing success. Bending to populist attacks on globalisation and the European Union begets the fundamental truth that it has never been possible to create 'social democracy in one country': today's world is more internationalised and interconnected than ever before. The greatest challenge for social democrats, however, remains the battle to sustain political coalitions in favour of collectivised social security and public provision in a world where structural change may be eroding the cross-class coalition in support of welfare states. This chapter has addressed which voters the left is losing; the chapter that follows will seek to explain precisely why social democratic parties across Europe appear to be performing so badly.

NOTES

1. G. Moschonas, 'Electoral Dynamics and Social Democratic Identity: Socialism and its changing constituencies in France, Great Britain, Sweden and Denmark'.
2. G. Moschonas, 'Electoral Dynamics and Social Democratic Identity'.

WHAT EXPLAINS THE POOR PERFORMANCE OF CENTRE-LEFT PARTIES?

It is well documented that since the financial crisis, European centre-left parties have performed poorly in elections. The previous chapter demonstrated that the support-base of social democratic parties has eroded significantly in recent decades, and the centre left can no longer rely on traditional class and political allegiances. But the reasons why social democrats have not performed effectively in elections go beyond the process of structural change and class de-alignment. There are a set of short-run and long-term factors which explain the centre left's anaemic performance since the 2008 financial crisis. The short-term factors relate to particular events and contingencies:

Economic credibility

The 2008 crisis destroyed the reputation of many centre-left governments for economic competence especially in countries such as Britain and Spain; they were in power when the crisis hit and social democrats had been associated with deregulatory policies and fiscal profligacy in the previous decade. Even in countries where the centre left was not in government, the economic crash did not produce any dramatic shift towards the left. The crisis highlighted the problems of inequality and disorderly financial markets, but voters more often yearned for stability and a 'safe pair of hands' rather than radical 'anti-austerity' policies. Social democrats were caught in an electoral bind: if they offered more austerity, voters could not tell the difference between them and the centre right. But if the centre-left appeared complacent about debt and public sector deficits, it faced electoral annihilation.

No money left

The fiscal aftershock of the economic crisis has in turn destroyed the traditional rationale of modernised social democracy: increased public spending and investment in infrastructure and the public realm. The question with which centre-left leaders are wrestling almost everywhere is what does social democracy stand for when there's no money left? The task of coalition building has become much tougher since parties can no longer dish out palliatives and electoral 'sweeteners' to key electoral groups.

Too few leaders

Across Europe, centre-left parties have recently had too few credible, persuasive leaders. They appear to lack a model of effective 'charismatic' leadership which can inspire voters while being honest about the challenges and trade-offs confronting politics in the real world. In many countries, traditional social democratic parties have maintained 'closed' selection processes which require successful politicians to advance through the party bureaucracy, working against more exciting 'insurgent' candidates with experience outside conventional political institutions.

Pasokification

The 'Pasokification' of European politics since 2008 has been significant, as the previous discussion showed. The rise of 'challenger parties' on left and right in many countries has repeatedly weakened the position of social democrats. Long-term changes in voting patterns and electoral systems have been attenuated by the impact of the crisis, which has forced voters to seek solutions on the radical margins of politics. From Scotland to Spain, traditional social democratic supporters have defected to left nationalist parties in protest against the perceived corruption of the democratic process.

The rise of 'compassionate Conservatism'

In reaction to the electoral dominance of social democratic parties in the late 1990s, centre-right parties have shifted pragmatically to the political centre, intensifying the electoral competition for social democrats where they confront new projects of 'compassionate Conservatism' notably in Germany, Sweden, and Britain. Christian democratic leaders such as Angela Merkel and Frederick Reinfeld have embraced traditional centre-left policies such as higher minimum wages and more generous welfare support for families. The new British prime minister, Theresa May, has made a similar bold move. The distinction between left and right appears less clear cut.

The fracturing of the European Union

Europe itself is weaker in the aftermath of the eurozone crisis, the decision of the UK on 23 June to withdraw from the EU, and uncertainty about the European project's future direction. Despite initial doubts about the Common Market and the single currency, social democrats in most countries have come to view the EU as an instrument to help achieve their political objectives, especially in social and environmental policy. Today, the European project is seemingly bereft: divisions over how to handle the migration crisis and the growing threat of terrorism force a retreat behind national borders. Voters perceive the EU as distant, bureaucratic and anti-democratic; parties respond by refusing to defend the European project. Euroscepticism is by no means confined to Britain. The weakening of political cooperation in Europe is perceived to be bad for social democracy.

Given these myriad problems, it is little wonder that social democrats have performed poorly in European elections over the last 15 years. Nonetheless, there are long-term challenges that have eroded the electoral position of centre-left parties since the 1960s and 1970s:

The death of class politics

The 'death' of class has made it tougher for social democrats to forge viable long-term electoral coalitions. As the previous chapter demonstrated, class still matters in the economy and society, but class no longer drives politics into monolithic blocs of 'working-class' and 'middle-class' voters. The process of structural de-alignment has been underway for over 50 years, eroding the capacity of social democrats to mobilise their electoral base. The third way sought an escape from this electoral dilemma by bringing middle-class voters firmly within the centre-left coalition; but the third way was unable to reconcile the 'materialist' orientation of its blue-collar working-class voters with the 'post-materialist' orientation of the post-1968 middle-classes (Callaghan, 2009).

Individualisation

Another long-term challenge has been individualisation. Industrial and post-industrial societies have become increasingly individualised since the second world war, disrupting the traditional ethic of collectivism that was once at the core of socialism and social democracy. The sociologist Ulrich Beck has illustrated the yearning for greater personal autonomy and freedom which has been underway in industrialised societies since the 1950s. The 1968 'social revolutions' confirmed the growth of post-materialist values in Europe which have cut against traditional forms of collectivist organisation.

Social democratic institutions under pressure

In the meantime, structural change has put greater pressure on traditional social democratic institutions, notably the welfare state and public services which have been in difficulty since the 1970s.

In the aftermath of the second world war, it was widely believed that economic growth would be sufficient to fund universal provision; demographic and technological changes have thrown this assumption into doubt. Greater longevity and growing demand from a more affluent population has increased the long-term cost pressures on the welfare state. Centre-left parties in power have often been slow to contemplate necessary structural reforms.

The 'hollowing-out' of democracy

The weakening of representative democracy as manifested in declining election turnouts and the 'hollowing out' of mass centre-left parties and trade unions has damaged social democracy. Historically, the rise of social democracy was predicated on the 'primacy of politics'. The centre-left no longer has the capacity to mobilise voters as it did immediately after 1945; the risk is that economically marginalised and younger voters are permanently disengaged from democratic institutions and representative politics.

The rise of identity politics

The growth of nationalism and identity politics has been uncomfortable for social democrats who have adopted a predominantly liberal cosmopolitan outlook. It forces these parties to make difficult choices about where to strike the balance in immigration policy; and it makes the centre left vulnerable to the drift of traditional social democratic supporters to the populist right, particularly in northern Europe. Where older nationalist enmities emerge such as in the UK and Spain, the risk is that the nation state breaks up in its existing form, disrupting traditional class alliances.

Have the 'old battles' been won?

Finally, social democracy may have been the victim of its own success since the 1950s and 1960s. Having forged an enduring postwar consensus followed by the social reforms of the 'permissive society' in the 1960s and the 1990s, there is less of a clamour for political change in most of the industrialised countries. The liberalisation of social and cultural attitudes has proceeded apace. Social democracy acquired its identity from the sense of righting wrongs and injustices in society; this is harder where the old 'giants' have been tackled, abolished or have just disappeared.

'NOSTALGIA' AND 'DESPAIR'

None of these developments have pre-determined consequences for centre-left politics; nor is there a 'golden age' which they should seek to re-capture; in reality, social democracy has always been tough going, including in the 1950s and 1960s where there were regularly economic and political crises. But social democratic parties have to adapt and change if they are not to remain electorally marginalised. This book warns against the widespread claim that history is stacked inexorably against the left, and that the long march of progress has gone into reverse (Gamble, 2010). Social democracy does face 'testing times' in Europe and across much of the world, but the pessimism can be overstated, lapsing into what Andrew Gamble terms the politics of 'nostalgia' and the politics of 'despair'.[1]

This interpretation of history is pervasive among many European social democrats: as Gamble states, it begins with the claim that third way social democracy has achieved little since the late 1980s, in the face of increasing acquiescence to neoliberalism. Many traditional social democratic values have apparently been abandoned, as governments everywhere seek to roll back the state. Having asserted social democracy's capitulation to economic liberalism, what follows inevitably are the politics of 'nostalgia' (Gamble, 2010). The period between 1945 and the early 1970s is hailed as a 'golden age', in which social democracy fought to entrench universal social citizenship encapsulated in the welfare state, and a model of regulated capitalism that protected citizens within the nation state from misfortune (Berman, 2006). In Britain, the postwar Attlee government is still regarded as the pinnacle of socialist achievement.

This narrative might appear politically persuasive, but it radically overstates the efficacy of neoliberalism during the 1980s, giving a false impression of social democratic durability during the years of the 'long boom' (Gamble, 2010; Callaghan, 2009). In the 1950s, for example, many western European countries were dominated by parties of the Christian democratic right, having skilfully captured the postwar settlement promising a new model of social market capitalism (Callaghan, 2009). It was only in Scandinavia that the centre left was capable of sustained electoral hegemony. Another weakness of the politics of nostalgia is that too much ground is conceded to the free market right. The ideology of neoliberalism became influential in the early 1980s, as the postwar settlement collapsed (Blyth, 2011). Indeed, many of its guiding assumptions live on, even in the wake of the 2008 financial crisis. But the state has hardly been rolled back or entirely dismantled, as the critics of third way politics commonly allege. Even in the UK, among the most 'neoliberal' of the western European countries, the struggle to rein in public expenditure after 1979 was far from successful (Taylor-Gooby, 2013). Welfare spending as a proportion of national income was substantially higher when the Conservatives left office in 1997; across the industrialised economies, expenditure on the welfare state and social protection as a proportion of GDP increased from 1980 to 2005 by more than six per cent (Gamble, 2010).

The fundamental weakness of the politics of 'despair' and the politics of 'nostalgia' is that they emphasise the defensive preservation of existing ideals and institutions, instead of engaging radically with the challenges of the future. Social democracy has to adjust to new challenges in order to address the needs of today's society; that requires deep reflection about the strategic aims and guiding purpose of centre-left politics (Gamble, 2010). The next chapter addresses that question directly by undertaking an assessment of the various governing programmes and strategies that social democrats have sought to develop in power since the late 1990s.

NOTE

1. A. Gamble, 'Social Democracy' on 'Social Europe', January 2010.

SOCIAL DEMOCRACY: A CRISIS OF IDEAS?

The argument of this book is that the centre left is losing elections since it has patently lacked a distinctive, compelling project for the future. Social democrats have become increasingly defensive, both intellectually and politically, as they see the political landscape around them changing in ways that are hardly propitious for the left. In Europe and the United States, the rise of new populist forces on both left and right appears to be dragging politics in ever more radical directions, 'hollowing out' the political territory on which social democratic parties once stood. The rise of left and right populism has made the politics of western democracies more 'noisy', but this turmoil often disguises the fact that the majority of voters still yearn for competent, stable and broadly progressive government. In this environment, the centre left has to re-discover the courage of its convictions while setting out a new vision.

SOCIAL DEMOCRACY AND THE THIRD WAY

The debate about ideas on the centre left often begins with discussion of third way social democracy, the now infamous effort to modernise social democracy during the 1990s. An increasingly fashionable argument since the 1960s and 1970s has been that ideas no longer matter in politics: we have entered an age of technocracy and rationalism signalling 'the end of ideology'. To some extent, this view underpinned the development of the third way. The third way's core proposition was that 'what matters is what works'; the practicality of policy and the results it generated mattered more than the ideological content of that policy. It was argued that social democrats had to break out of the conventional boundaries that traditionally separated left and right. Supporters of the third way insisted that this was a necessary act of 'revisionism', updating social democracy for changing times; but the third way's opponents countered that centre-left parties were being shorn of their ideological convictions. This was more resonant in the aftermath of the financial crisis in 2008–9, when centre-left parties were held to be culpable for inadequate regulatory oversight of financial markets while tolerating huge rises in economic inequality.

It is striking that in the late 1990s there was a wave of enthusiasm about the revival of progressive parties in US and European politics; however, this was accompanied by much debate, and perhaps even confusion, about whether electoral success would be translated into more profound social change (White, 1999). Rather than furthering progressive commitments to egalitarian reform, social justice, political freedom, and the extension of democratic governance, the perception was that many third way governments merely tinkered with an established Conservative settlement initiated by Ronald Reagan and Margaret Thatcher in the early 1980s (Gamble, 2010). In the US, Clinton's New Democrats confounded the hopes of many progressive liberals by appearing to pander to a conservative agenda in order to secure re-election (Weir, 1999). In countries such as Britain and Germany, Tony Blair and Gerhard Schröder were regarded as the agents of a pro-market reform agenda under the guise of 'modernising' social democracy.

It can be legitimately argued that the core project of third way politics was a genuine response not only to the shattering of the post-1945 Keynesian settlement, but to structural changes that have occurred since the demise of the postwar social contract in the late 1970s. In the economy, dramatic changes were underway as a result of the internationalisation of capital markets and the expansion of world trade; the rise of information and communications technologies; the emergence of a 'knowledge-driven economy'; and the shift from manufacturing to services that heralded a 'post-industrial economy' in the west (Callaghan, 2009). These economic forces interacted with important social changes, notably the fragmentation of traditional class structures; changes in the position of women reflected in growing labour force participation; demographic changes such as population ageing and the acceleration of labour migration; the apparent breakdown of traditional family structures; as well as an alarming decline of trust in democracy and government (Esping-Andersen, 2009).

In fact, many of the changes represented 'opportunities' as much as 'threats' for left parties; notably they instigated an unfinished feminisation process within social democracy which brought concerns about gender equality to the forefront of politics: there was no process of inexorable structural decline. The prediction that social democratic parties were doomed to defeat because of changes in the class structure proved to be exaggerated. Nonetheless, such developments made it harder to build a stable, cross-class alliance to match the power of organised labour in the 1950s and 1960s, the halcyon days of the postwar welfare state (Cronin, Ross & Schoch, 2010). The constraints imposed by globalisation, increasing welfare dependency, and declining faith in government appeared to circumscribe what social democratic parties were able to achieve in office. Indeed, the shift towards more dynamic and volatile 'issues-based' politics combined with the growing importance of perceived governmental competence and performance have created a febrile environment for governing parties of all ideological complexions (Stoker, 2006).

The third way was a concerted attempt to rethink social democratic politics in the wake of the Thatcher-Reagan hegemony, alongside the apparent dominance of 'neoliberal' ideas in advanced capitalist democracies. Numerous critics have sought to subject the third way to extensive critique since the mid-1990s. For instance, academics such as Chris Pierson (2001) insist that the third way had overstated the impact of economic and social change especially that associated with globalisation. In a similar vein, Ashley Lavelle (2008) argues that the third way entailed an unnecessary degree of accommodation with neoliberalism. The terrain of a distinctive left political economy centred on market intervention was prematurely abandoned. Marcus Ryner (2010), benefiting from the hindsight afforded by the 2008–9 financial crash, avers that New Labour's model of social democracy meant a 'Faustian' bargain with market liberalism. The legacy was growing income inequality and an economy dangerously unbalanced by financialisation. Finally, the Swedish political scientist Jenny Andersson (2009) observes that third way social democracy entailed an emphasis on the rise of the 'knowledge-driven economy', which justified a new compromise between the private sector, workers and the state unified by the goal of widening access to human capital. Andersson concludes that the third way assimilates all forms of human potential and the public good under the rubric of economic growth and higher productivity, aiding the remorseless process of commodification in capitalist societies.

Other important structural changes in the 'Anglo-Saxon' economies were also downplayed or ignored by the third way. These included the substantial increase in earnings and income inequality in many western countries; the growing concentration of wealth among the richest one per cent of the population; the growth of relative poverty (especially child poverty); persistently high rates of economic inactivity among the unskilled (especially in the UK and some continental European states); as well as the emergence of excluded minorities economically and geographically isolated from the economic and social mainstream. The third way confronted a core paradox: economic and social change was generating new demands for progressive intervention by the state; at the same time, these very forces were eroding and undermining citizen's trust in government, which manifested itself in declining election turnouts and growing disillusionment with the political process. Social democracy struggled to reconcile its aspirational rhetoric centred on social justice and the equal worth of all with the economic and political realities imposed by governing a liberal capitalist economy.

Moreover, the third way implicitly assumed that social democratic parties would converge around a single model of centre-left governance; but there have always been strikingly divergent national pathways within social democracy: there are distinctive models of British, French, German and Nordic centre-left politics. More recently, the British model has accepted globalisation and flexibility in capital and labour markets tempered by ameliorative government intervention. The German centre left has undertaken liberalising reforms since the late 1990s, but preserved the corporatist model of tripartite cooperation between employers, trade unions and the state. Similarly, the Nordic social democratic parties have remained open to globalisation and free trade, but have embedded the traditional pillars of the Scandinavian model such as collective wage bargaining and a relatively high density of trade union membership. Finally, the socialists in France have accepted some reforms of the state's role in the economy, but the French left remains committed to achieving a high level of social protection through government regulation and intervention. This point underlines that there have always been 'multiple third ways' for social democracy in Europe.

Neither are the various criticisms of the third way always convincing: for example, Ben Clift and Jim Tomlinson (2007) have taken issue with the claim that UK centre-left modernisation in the late 1990s meant the abandonment of postwar Keynesian social democracy. For one, previous British social democratic governments in the 1940s and the 1960s had never been avowedly Keynesian: they were committed to nationalisation, more interested in economic planning, and rather distrustful of Keynesian theories which sought to defend the legitimacy of the liberal market economy. New Labour did not abandon demand-management but combined it with supply-side policies; the pursuit of 'credibility' was intended to create more space for fiscal activism as public spending grew markedly as a share of GDP after 1998–9; indeed, the Blair-Brown governments were fundamentally committed to the quintessentially Keynesian goal of full employment (Clift & Tomlinson, 2007: 66–69).

Moreover, for all the intellectual critiques of the third way, the pro-
longed attempt to 'modernise' social democracy was a serious effort
to rejuvenate centre-left ideas. The economic crisis and the imposition of austerity in the wake of the great recession have underlined
that ideas matter in politics. Ideas create 'cognitive frameworks'
which are the precondition for political and policy action, as Mark
Blyth (2011) has pointed out. It is ideas that enable social democratic parties to forge new coalitions for change, breaking down the
influence of vested interests. As John Maynard Keynes famously
remarked, 'The ideas of economists and political philosophers, both
when they are right and when they are wrong are more powerful than
is commonly understood. Indeed, the world is ruled by little else'.[1]

In revising the third way since the 1990s, social democrats in
Europe have developed three distinctive frameworks of ideas that
are briefly reviewed in the chapter below: first, the turn towards
'communitarianism' associated with Blue Labour in Britain; second,
the reassertion of a nascent version of cosmopolitan liberalism; and
finally, the call for a renewed attack on economic inequality on the
left.

THE COMMUNITARIAN TURN: 'MAKING SENSE OF BLUE LABOUR'

Communitarianism is a plural political ideology with roots both on
left and right. The set of ideas known as Blue Labour have dominated internal debate within the British Labour party since its devastating 2010 defeat, among the worst the party has suffered since
1918. Similarly, in the Netherlands and Germany there has been a
growing interest in communitarian ideas among social democrats,
partly in reaction to heightened concerns about the long-term impact
of migration on solidarity and community.

Election defeats have triggered an inevitable period of soul-search-
ing, the most tangible product of which has been the Blue Labour
prospectus. This occurred in the absence of any serious intellectual

contribution either from the organised left or the remnants of New Labour. Exponents of Blue Labour expressed their ideas in the language of 'love, community, neighbourliness, fraternity, relationships and the common good'. This was unusual in British politics, while leading Blue Labour exponents made a series of controversial claims. Maurice Glasman, widely viewed as Blue Labour's leading intellectual voice, argued that the Labour governments had been dishonest about their intensions in liberalising immigration policy and accepting free movement of labour, as they feared a backlash from voters. Glasman was appointed to the House of Lords in 2011 by Ed Miliband, then Labour leader; his views have been taken seriously by the British media and the political class.

Blue Labour did not just provide a critique of immigration policy, but entailed a commitment to reclaiming past traditions, including respect for working-class life and the values of solidarity and collectivism that once animated the British left. The prefix 'blue' indicates a residual sympathy towards conservatism as a philosophy, not to be confused with the British Conservative *party,* which remains avowedly free market; it speaks to an appetite in the country to protect, safeguard, and improve the vital aspects of our common life, in particular England's language, culture and institutions (Rutherford, 2010). Blue Labour embodies several important strands in the Labour tradition. It is a complex amalgam of distinctive ideological and intellectual tendencies which shares certain similarities with earlier phases of Labour party thought, namely the ethical socialism of Ramsay MacDonald and RH Tawney; the commitment of Clement Attlee's Labour to a democratic 'common culture' in the postwar years; the pragmatic labourism of Harold Wilson and James Callaghan in the 1960s and 1970s; alongside the distinctive communitarianism and ethical socialism of the Blair years prior to 1997 (Rutherford, 2010).

Blue Labour involves an array of diverse and distinct positions. For example, Glasman is a strong exponent of the politics of virtue and the common good rooted in the social teaching of faith communities. Others emphasise the importance of Labour rediscovering its commitment to a democratic 'common life'. The cultural theorist Jonathan Rutherford (2010) draws attention to the importance of rooting politics in everyday lived experience, particularly the parochialism of England, English culture and English identity. However, what unifies Blue Labour is its resistance to the commodification of human beings through markets, which allegedly strips life of all that is intrinsically valuable, echoing the early writings of Karl Marx and Georg Wilhelm Friedrich Hegel. Their most inspirational theorist is Karl Polanyi who has shaped the thinking of Glasman in particular, by examining the impact of capitalist markets on 17th and 18th century England. The process of commodification has been intensified in the 21st century by New Labour's commitment to a 'dynamic knowledge-based economy' driven by globalisation. Unlike other anti-capitalist movements, Blue Labour sees capitalism as a problem not of class exploitation or structural inequality, but primarily of commodification and the unruly forces of capital (Glasman, 2010). The aim of left politics ought to be to resist the forces of marketisation that transform individual citizens into commodities.

In policy terms, Blue Labour embraces 'stakeholder' economics, redirecting British capitalism from its Anglo-American orientation towards northern European models centred on German and Scandinavian experience. In practice, that means a commitment to corporatism involving workplace partnership between employers and the workforce; altering the culture of mergers and takeovers; restraining executive remuneration; as well as curtailing the 'hire and fire' culture of the American labour market. It entails much greater emphasis on vocational skills and training, celebrating the permanence of 'craft and vocation' rather than endlessly flexible human capital. Another aspect of its economic model is the localisation of political authority and power through city government, alongside the regionalisation of the banking system.

Most European social democrats would regard this as a mainstream centre-left programme. Blue Labour has been a constructive exercise in mapping out and framing a distinctive social democratic project in the wake of the global financial crisis. Nonetheless, the overall coherence of Blue Labour remains doubtful. The most important weaknesses relate to class identity; the risk of parochialism; and the absence of a plausible account of political agency.

Blue Labour exponents have been right to draw attention to the continuing relevance of class as a marker of economic and political identity. New Labour may have gone too far in abandoning the party's historic role as an agent of working-class solidarity and collective organisation. Nonetheless, it can hardly be doubted that class has ceased to play the role that it once did in British political life, and Labour's response to this was a necessary precondition for electoral recovery in the 1990s. In the first half of the 20th century, individuals (predominantly men) understood their position in terms of their status as producers and workers. Today, the role of 'consumers' is a far more prevalent aspect of social and political identity; centre-left politics has had to come to terms with the rise of the consumer society (Callaghan, 2009). The left might decry these historical developments, but the failure to comprehend the rise of affluence and consumerism has been politically costly. Even more to the point, the manual working class has shrunk dramatically in size across almost all advanced economies, and is no longer in a position to propel social democratic parties to victory.

A further vulnerability within Blue Labour's ideology is that of parochialism (Runciman, 2013). The desire to re-galvanise local places and the spirit of community is legitimate, but the reality of global interdependence is hard to refute given the growing importance of globalised production chains. Liberal cosmopolitanism may have its weaknesses, not least alienating those who have failed to gain from the globalisation of economic production, but 'socialism in one country' has scarcely appeared credible since the 1960s and 1970s. Any social democratic government is constrained by international markets alongside dependency on overseas investors and foreign capital. It is far from obvious that international market forces can be resisted by exerting the nation state's power as a sovereign actor. What is lacking from Blue Labour is an account of political agency, of how desired changes are to be brought about given the obstacles imposed by existing political and economic realities. The risk for its exponents is of falling into a traditional void: failing to reconcile a radical form of rhetoric with the practical means to fulfil Blue Labour's vision of a fairer, more equal society.

LIBERALISM AND SOCIAL DEMOCRACY

If Blue Labour and social conservatism is not wholly the answer, should the left reclaim the social liberal tradition? In particular, the American political tradition centred on faith in progressive liberalism has long provided social democrats in Europe with ideas and ideological inspiration. This extends from Theodore Roosevelt's progressive reform movement at the turn of the 20th century, to Franklin Delano Roosevelt's New Deal in the 1930s, through to Lyndon Johnson's 1960s Great Society, and the 'New Democrat' fusion of fiscal responsibility and social liberalism under Bill Clinton in the 1990s. At the core of that tradition is a belief in an ethic of liberalism underpinned by the notion of 'positive freedom': the idea that citizens will fulfil themselves not merely by achieving liberty from external constraint, but by having the power and resources to fulfil their full potential. Positive liberty is enhanced by the ability of citizens to participate in their government and civil society, and to have their voice, interests and concerns recognised as valid and acted upon (White, 1999). This is at the root of the enduring vision of economic and social progress provided by progressive liberalism in the US.

The relationship between liberalism and social democracy has long been contested, particularly among parties of the left who sought to differentiate European socialism from American liberalism (Sassoon, 1996). Nonetheless, notions of civil rights, democratic accountability, personal liberty, and civic duty have remained influential. Throughout history, socialists and social democrats have sought to temper their faith in the power of government by recognising the importance of protecting citizens from overweening concentrations of power, investing in institutions and policies that would enable citizens to flourish regardless of background or birth.

At root, social democratic and socialist parties in western Europe have long drawn strength from their immersion in liberal traditions and ideological lineages (Freeden, 1978).

Today, the contribution of progressive liberalism to the contemporary political debate appears questionable. On both sides of the Atlantic, centre-left parties are struggling to establish a clear ideological direction in the wake of the financial crisis. Since the collapse of Lehman Brothers in 2008, social democrats in the European Union have lost 26 out of 33 national elections. In Britain, Germany and Sweden, the left has experienced among the worst defeats in its history. The challenge for those of a progressive temperament is to come to terms with the collapse of faith both in markets and the state in the wake of the financial crisis. The death of neoliberalism has been widely proclaimed[2], but few varieties or models of capitalism have appeared to fill the void created by the collapse of confidence in financialised capitalism.

The crisis has evolved from a crisis of global financial markets, to a crisis in the international banking system, to a crisis of sovereign debt, to a wider crisis of declining trust in governments and the democratic system (Gamble, 2012). This alludes to a deep crisis of legitimacy and trust in liberal democracy in the advanced industrialised nations. In domestic politics, at exactly the moment when stagnating economic growth is squeezing living standards and the revenues available for public investment, faith in the democratic institutions that are intended to ensure a fair distribution of the burdens of austerity is receding. Citizens are equally perplexed by the consequences of globalisation: on the one hand, they want to be protected from the myriad insecurities unleashed by the free movement of goods, services and finance. On the other hand, they seek greater choice and control over their lives, and remain suspicious of an overmighty, centralising state (Mulgan, 2005). It is no surprise that questions of identity, nationhood and belonging have returned to the fore of contemporary politics.

This is the context in which 21st century progressive movements have to rediscover their political vitality and sense of ideological purpose. This book considers whether re-engagement between the American and European progressive traditions can help to forge new doctrines, narratives, and strategies that have the potential to inaugurate a paradigm shift beyond neoliberalism in the advanced democracies, while providing the resources through which to affect a broader recovery in the fortunes of social democratic politics.

Social liberalism and the future

It might be argued that social liberalism is therefore of little relevance to the contemporary political context given its embrace of free markets and complacency about rising inequalities. Social liberalism merely replicates the weaknesses of the third way approaches already alluded to. Critics have suggested that social liberalism has repeatedly ignored or understated the potential for state intervention and non-market coordination. Social liberalism is portrayed as concerned with ensuring that citizens have roughly equal starting points, but then allowing the market to run its course (White, 1999). It is argued that there is little to distinguish social liberalism from neoliberalism. The third way version of social liberalism was said to have been oblivious to the range of institutional legacies that different progressive and social democratic parties have faced, and the extent to which they have been able to draw upon, and develop, social liberal ideas in power (Weir, 1999). Nonetheless, while it might appear that social liberalism has little to offer social democracy in the wake of the economic crash – a crisis which the left believed might allow the return of the centralised state to the centre of policy debate – that conclusion has turned out to be misplaced. For instance:

- Social liberals have always stressed the potential for market failure, privileging neither the state nor market instruments; they argue for the pragmatic integration of state and non-state actors in the economy, including the strengthening of the mutual and not-for-profit sector (White, 1999).
- Progressive liberals have long acknowledged that they have no alternative but to periodically revise their programmes in the light of the changing nature of capitalism. They have also accepted the

need to face up to the dilemmas implicit in the trade-off between economic efficiency and social justice (Meade, 1993).

- Social liberals have affirmed a major role for the state both in tempering the earnings inequalities that labour markets create through the minimum wage and skills policies; and by developing programmes through which risks can be pooled in order to meet responsibilities such as caring, as well as life course needs (Esping-Andersen, 1999).

- Social liberalism seeks to alter the distribution of assets that citizens bring to the market through 'social investment' strategies (Jenson & Saint-Martin, 2003). Social liberalism is perfectly compatible with a conception of 'strong egalitarianism'. The problem since the late 1990s was that many third way governments lacked strategies that would end the entrapment of low-waged workers in poor quality jobs, or that challenged the low-wage, low-productivity 'disequilibrium' in Anglo-Saxon economies.

- A number of liberal economists and political theorists have explored the potential for 'asset-based egalitarianism' to improve the equity/efficiency trade-off in market economies. Such proposals have included universal capital endowments financed through inheritance tax, and a citizen's income funded through public investment in capital markets (White, 1999).

- A liberal public philosophy remains important for negotiating contemporary policy dilemmas, not least democratic governance reform, anxieties about immigration management, civil liberties, community cohesion, and issues relating to the rights and duties of citizens (Weir, 1999). A central thrust as Margaret Weir argues is that means must be found to encourage citizens to engage and participate in the political process. The debate between 'liberal' and 'communitarian' conceptions of civic responsibility can help to clarify the underlying purpose of progressive policy initiatives.

Progressive left parties ought to consider how to unlock new 'political opportunity structures' given the growing fragmentation and fluidity of politics (Cronin, Ross & Schoch, 2010). Reconsidering the relationship between social liberalism and social democracy ought to be integral to that process. What is required is a vigorous development of the 'new' liberalism that emerged at the turn of the 20th century, with its roots in a broader tradition of democratic and social republicanism stretching back to figures such as LT Hobhouse, TH Green and Thomas Paine (Freeden, 1978). This is a reminder that liberalism was once a popular movement anchored in working-class institutions across civil society – the trade unions, friendly societies, worker's education, and the chapel. It is worrying that over time, the civic institutions of progressivism have been allowed to atrophy and decline (Rutherford, 2014). The task today is less about inventing an entirely novel approach to 'liberal' social democracy. Instead we ought to be concerned with drawing on, and re-appropriating, these rich traditions and narratives in order to engage more forcefully with the challenges of the present (Gamble, 2010).

INEQUALITY

In contradistinction to reclaiming a lost social liberalism, others on the left advocate a renewed offensive against inequality. It is claimed the fight against inequality ought to be the lodestar of the left, but we need to be clear both about what causes inequality, and more importantly, what constitutes social justice and equality today. For generations, political theorists have struggled to formulate a convincing conception of the egalitarian ideal.

In the debate about what creates economic inequality, a host of factors have been cited in a burgeoning literature (Taylor-Gooby, 2013). Rising immigration is one driver. Declining rates of unionisa-tion is another. Both are believed to have weakened the bargaining power of low-skilled workers, alongside the fall in the relative value of the national minimum wage in many countries. Another factor is the growth of international trade and the globalisation of labour, product and capital markets since the 1980s: as the balance of eco-nomic advantage shifts to the east, many jobs in the west become uncompetitive or obsolete. Each of these explanations has received considerable attention from politicians and policymakers. This is hardly surprising since there is evidence that these factors have each contributed to the sharp rise in inequality of income and wages, especially in the US and the UK.

According to research presented by Alan Krueger, one of US president Barack Obama's economic advisers, the most important driver of economic inequality is 'skill-biased' technological change, as Figure 4.1 makes clear. This increases the number of relatively skilled jobs at the top of the labour market, while skewing the wage distribution towards those with the highest levels of human capital (Goos & Manning, 2014). There is considerable debate within the economics profession about the impact of technological change, but it is unquestionably a potent driver of inequality mediated by education and skills. The OECD has recently predicted that jobs requiring 'highly educated workers' will rise by 20 per cent in the next decade across the advanced economies, whereas low-skilled jobs are likely to fall by more than 10 per cent.

Moreover, low-skilled workers are increasingly vulnerable to the threat of redundancy and unemployment in a period of ongoing

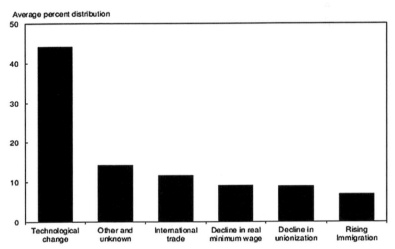

Figure 4.1 Causes of Earnings Inequality. *Source*: Economic Report of the President, 1997

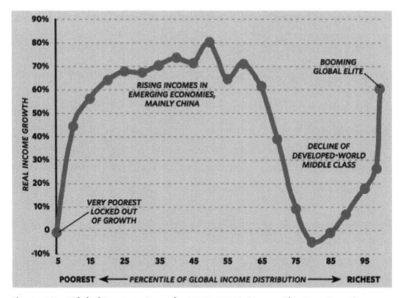

Figure 4.2   Global Income Growth, 1988–2008. *Source*: The American Prospect, using data provided by Branko Milanovic[3]

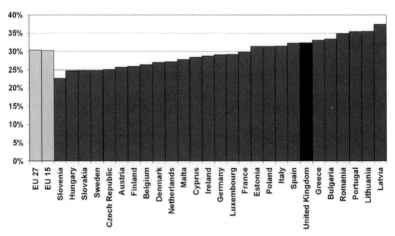

Figure 4.3   Income Inequality: Gini Coefficient. *Source*: EU Community Statistics on Income and Living Conditions; the data is for 2009; updated December 2010

economic restructuring. In the EU28 countries, 84 per cent of working-age adults with 'higher' (tertiary level) skills are currently working compared to less than half of those with low skills (Sage et al, 2015). Downward pressure on wages and fear of unemployment is leading to heightened economic insecurity for those on lower and middle incomes. Across the OECD, median income households have experienced a much sharper decline in incomes than was the case 30 years ago.

The whole of Europe has clearly been afflicted in recent decades by rising inequalities. But work by Branko Milanović which produced the famously termed 'elephant curve' demonstrates more precisely who has gained and who has lost out across the income distribution in the global economy, as shown in Figure 4.2. In summary, the poor in developing countries who three decades ago lived in abject poverty have gained significantly from global economic integration. The 'losers' have been middle-class groups in already rich countries who have lost out in the income distribution compared to the wealthy minority: Milanović's argument is that the forces driving inequality in both industrialised and developing states are resolutely global, yet the policy response to inequality remains predominantly national.[4] This should serve as a warning to those who believe that Britain's withdrawal from the EU is likely to produce gains in income and wealth equality over the coming decades. Meanwhile, Figure 4.3 illustrates the prevalence of inequality across the EU as measured by the Gini co-efficient.

As Milanović's work underlines, structural trends in the global economy have led to substantive inequalities in the wage and income distribution in rich market democracies, attenuated by the crisis of 2008–9. At the same time, governments have been less effective at mitigating the risks increasingly associated with global economic integration and openness to the world economy. A paper published by the economist Dani Rodrik in the late 1990s illustrates the point: at the beginning of the 1990s Rodrik (1998: 997) found that in countries that were more exposed to global trade such as

Norway, Sweden and Austria, the size of government expenditure was greater. His explanation: public spending is used to insure citizens against increasing external risk; in the advanced capitalist countries, government expenditure on welfare and social security protects individuals against volatility in employment, incomes and consumption. From this, we can see how two particular problems have arisen in EU member states since the financial crisis. First, the union was predicated on a 'division of labour' in which the EU is a force for liberalisation through the single market, while it is nation states that protect citizens from external risk given the underdeveloped social dimension of Europe. The increasing inability of national governments to perform this role given escalating public sector deficits since 2008 has imperilled the EU as a political project. Second, the inability of governments to constrain the impact of global economic integration through 'risk-mitigating' expenditures illustrates the growing structural divergence between politics and markets. The historical role of social democracy was to better reconcile markets with politics to reduce class conflict and to foster democratic stability: it is little wonder that centre-left parties are increasingly on the back-foot.

Moreover, governments at all levels have struggled to live up to the challenge of equipping individuals to face new uncertainties in their working lives, coping with risks such as obsolete skills and inadequate education. Nearly one in seven (around 78 million people in Europe) are at risk of poverty; shockingly, child poverty has continued to rise across member states over the last decade (Esping-Andersen, 2009). Children (0–17) have a particularly high rate of poverty at 19 per cent. One-parent households and those with dependent children have the highest poverty risk; for single parents with one dependent child, the risk is currently 33 per cent; other age groups at a high risk of poverty are young people (18–24) at 18 per cent, and older people (65+) at 19 per cent; older women are at a considerably higher risk than men (21 per cent compared to 16 per cent) (Sage et al, 2015). As highlighted earlier, these figures do not include some of those in the most extreme situations, particularly ethnic minority groups. Of course, poverty rates are notably only one dimension of social injustice, and inequality.

Welfare states have arguably placed too much emphasis on passive income redistribution and 'insider' guarantees of social protection, without helping to equip Europe's citizens for the competitive challenges of the future. The more recent labour market research demonstrates that wage inequality in Europe has intensified since the late 1990s: while income redistribution has been strengthened, labour market regulation and wage protection have eased (Goos & Manning, 2014). This has, in turn, fuelled the legitimacy crisis facing the EU, which is increasingly blamed for the negative consequences of globalisation, liberalisation and austerity.

The main drivers of growing inequality inevitably vary across the Europe continent. In the core continental member states, slow growth and rising unemployment have been a particular challenge for the last three decades. For the 10 member states that joined the EU in 2004, including the eight former communist countries, this has been a fraught period of transition and adjustment; for the 'periphery' countries, namely Ireland, Portugal, Greece and Spain, there has been a phase of rapid modernisation, at least until the financial collapse of 2008–9 (Sage et al, 2015). In contrast, the Nordic countries have developed social models that led to outstanding growth performance since the early 1990s.[5] It might be expected that these factors are reflected in public attitudes to the varying dimensions of social justice.

At the same time, while there is great diversity *between*, as well as *within*, countries, all member states face common challenges such as demography, increased ethnic and cultural diversity, and the individualisation of values (Lerais & Liddle, 2006). Every member state in the EU is a relatively open society shaped by the forces of international capital, alongside global cultural trends and values. In many societies, there is an increasing cultural gap between 'cosmopolitans' who are portrayed as the 'winners' of globalisation and social change, and those who are left behind through the economic transition, perceiving their traditional values, neighbourhoods and sense of belonging to be under threat (Callaghan, 2009). This new divide between 'liberals' and 'communitarians' forms an important backdrop to public attitudes in relation to social justice.

CRISIS AFTERSHOCKS AND THE NEW INEQUALITIES

Social democrats also need to understand how the world is changing to increase inequality and polarisation: 'crisis aftershocks' since 2008 have made it tougher to carry out social democratic programmes in pursuit of equality and social justice across Europe. First, current crisis aftershocks originate in long-term structural trends relating to demography, life expectancy, globalisation, and the changing shape of the productive economy in the west, not just the financial crash itself (Sapir, 2014). These trends are common across the EU's member states, despite their different stages of economic development. In some respects they have been exacerbated by the global shocks of 2008–09 as Andre Sapir has argued, which has underlined the global shift in economic power away from Europe and the rest of the developed world, as shown by the remarkable resilience of the emerging Asian economies. By contrast, the consequences of the shock to growth and the public spending consequences of the financial crisis will make it harder to address long-term social and economic challenges. Many European governments struggled to implement immediate crisis management measures, and have had to deal with the fallout of the sovereign debt crisis. In the meantime, hastily conceived fiscal austerity measures have had a major impact. The danger is that during an era of fiscal retrenchment, existing welfare policy regimes will be frozen as governments struggle to reassure citizens and protect people from the adverse consequences of the crisis. It is precisely at this moment, however, that reform is needed most, not only to manage new financial pressures, but to make welfare states more resilient for the future and prevent the crisis from further damaging the life chances of the least advantaged in society.

These crisis aftershocks have nonetheless put social and economic inequality back at the centre of the public policy agenda. In a recent book, *The Spirit Level*, Richard Wilkinson and Kate Pickett show that unequal societies do far worse on a range of important social indicators including crime rates, public health, educational achievement, work-life balance, personal wellbeing, and so on. Thomas Picketty's work has demonstrated that the rate of return on capital exceeds the growth in wages in capitalist economies, leading to a long-term rise of inequality. Of course, the inequality debate has become broader than the traditional focus on economic inequality and the relationship between the top and bottom of the distribution. A new focus relates to the stagnation of the 'squeezed middle' and the downward pressure on their living standards created both by globalisation, and internally driven pressures such as deregulatory labour market reforms undertaken with the objective of raising employment participation rates (Sapir, 2014). The question of inequality cannot be separated from the wider debate about the nature of capitalism in the west, which has led to the revival of interest in the German coordinated social market economy regime, and the successes of globally orientated Nordic social democracy in combining efficiency and equity.

The final argument concerns the capacity of the European Union to present itself as a strategic actor well-placed to deal with the fallout of crisis aftershocks, helping to facilitate the return of Europe's economy and welfare regimes to stability and good health. This optimistic view of the EU's potential underestimates the extent to which the EU itself has accentuated the scale of the social inequalities facing member states principally through the dynamics of the internal market (Sage et al, 2015). Combined with EU enlargement, the single market has contributed to the increasingly adverse fortunes of the low skilled in the labour market and the erosion of labour standards. There is also the issue of whether the established EU policy framework, with its emphasis on fiscal discipline, national competitiveness and labour market reforms has contributed to the rise of zero-sum competition between member states (Sapir, 2014). Whereas before the crisis social policy experts imagined that membership of the EU contributed to a positive 'race to the top' for its national welfare states, the real impact of the crisis has been to exacerbate economic and social divergence in Europe, as member states find themselves with widely differing room for manoeuvre and therefore seeking different remedies to the challenges presented by the crisis (Sage et al, 2015). The ethic of solidarity between EU countries is weakened as a result. The basic legitimacy of the EU is put into question. Maurizio Ferrera has examined how national welfare states within the EU operate both within a clearly defined 'European economic space' as well as a more imprecise 'European social space', the parameters of which could now be altered, not least as the application of the new social provisions of the Lisbon treaty unfolds.

As a result of these changes, a growing 'social justice deficit' exists across Europe:

- Full employment no longer exists in most member states. In France, unemployment has hovered around 10 per cent for the best part of two decades with over a quarter of young people unable to find jobs. Even high-employment countries like the Netherlands, Sweden and the UK continue to have serious problems of working-age inactivity, in particular the number of claimants for sickness and invalidity benefits (Lerais & Liddle, 2006).
- Security against social risks is now partial. Welfare systems insured more or less successfully against the risks of 19th century industrialisation (unemployment, sickness, industrial injury and poverty in old age) with some gaps in countries which saw the family as taking full responsibility for young people for example. But European welfare states have found it more difficult to insure against the new social risks of modern life (single parenthood, relationship breakdown, mental illness, extreme frailty and incapacity in old age).
- Fairness between the generations has broken down. Pensioners have done relatively well, and the problem of poverty in old age is more confined to the new member states. However, child poverty

is a major issue in several European countries. In others young people bear the brunt of unemployment and fiscal retrenchment.

- The quality of public services in many continental countries is beginning to decline after years of public spending restraint created by slower growth. Many member states have an endowment of high-quality infrastructure built in a more economically dynamic era, but this will increasingly fray at the edges if growth remains slow and public finances tight.

- The industrial relations system that was supposed to guarantee fair treatment at work no longer protects the 'weak' against the 'powerful'. Some groups are well-protected as a result of social partnership, strong trade unions, collective agreements and legally enforceable employee rights, but they are privileged because they do not represent the majority of the workforce and those excluded from it. There is an increasing 'insider'/'outsider' division in European labour markets (Sapir, 2014).

- Most Europeans favour a society that leans against inequalities, although political parties differ about the degree of inequality they find tolerable. Inequalities are, in fact, growing in most member states as the result of higher rewards at the top as well as greater employment inactivity and low wages at the bottom. Inequalities in income and wealth are politically contested. However, the commonly-held aspiration that 'every child should have an equal chance in life' is less in reach than a generation ago; the disadvantages of social inheritance are becoming more embedded (Esping-Andersen, 1999; Sage et al, 2015).

Neither 'pure' equality of outcome nor 'radical' meritocracy

Social justice and equality have been the animating ideals of European social democracy for much of the last century. They reflect the core commitment of the centre left to *substantive* freedom, not only access to basic liberties and the right to self-determination, but

the ability to exercise individual autonomy through the opportunity
and security afforded by an active and enabling state. The role of
government is not to act as a barrier to freedom, but to enable and
enrich personal liberty. Nonetheless, despite their evident political
resonance in social democratic parties, social justice and equality
are ambiguous and contested concepts, with varying degrees of
purchase both *within* and *between* European societies. Equality
in particular has been attacked as representing 'levelling down'
through indiscriminate redistribution and punitive rates of income
tax. For that reason, many social democrats have preferred to
highlight their commitment to 'social justice'; the political theorist
David Miller has identified four pre-eminent dimensions of social
justice:[6]

- *Equal citizenship*: every citizen is entitled to civil, political and
  social rights including the means to exercise those rights effectively.
- *The social minimum*: all citizens must have access to resources
  that adequately meet their essential needs, and allow them to live
  a secure and dignified life in today's society.
- *Equality of opportunity*: an individual's life chances, especially
  their access to jobs and educational opportunities, should depend
  on their own motivation and aptitudes, not on irrelevant markers
  of difference such as gender, class or ethnicity.
- *Fair distribution*: resources that do not form part of equal citizenship or the social minimum may be distributed unequally, but
  the distribution must reflect 'legitimate criteria' such as personal
  desert, effort and genuine risk-taking rather than gaming economic
  rents through monopolistic markets (Miller, 1994: 31–36).

Miller's aim was to identify the core principles citizens use
to judge whether their societies are just or unjust. Of course, it
might be argued that Miller's list is deficient or at least inadequate.
The principle of equality of opportunity does not explicitly take
account of increasingly important intergenerational inequalities,
particularly in the light of climate change and its impact on future

generations, as well as de facto redistribution towards older citizens and retirees. At the same time, Miller's conception of social justice is framed in terms of rights and entitlements; he has relatively little to say about reciprocity and civic responsibility, the mutual obligations and duties that bind together political communities. Another gap in Miller's account relates to power: any persuasive account of social justice should capture the importance of giving individuals the power to shape their own lives, rather than being held back by the destiny of circumstances or birth.

Miller's framework undoubtedly offers an engaging and fruitful starting point for debate about the core purpose of social democracy. However, developing abstract understandings of social justice is plainly inadequate. As Peter Taylor-Gooby (2012) has indicated, it is necessary to understand the complexity of public attitudes, how public policy can work with the grain of public views, and where political parties might need to challenge the attitudes of voters. The evidence suggests that the public do not conceive social justice in terms of grand theories, but tend to relate conceptions of justice to specific life events, contexts and particularities (Mulgan, 2005). This is an important reminder to politicians; to capture the public's imagination they must relate their values to specific and tangible policy goals, rather than to intangible theoretical principles. The role of political theory is to help frame the narrative and discourse of social justice on which politicians can subsequently draw.

Attitudes do matter, not least because the literature indicates that how the public perceives inequality, poverty and the income distribution are an important aspect of a country's 'welfare culture' (Lepianka, Van Oorschot & Gelissen, 2009). These perceptions shape both the perceived legitimacy of particular welfare programmes, but also the overall shape and design of the welfare state. An important distinction is emphasised between those countries where poverty tends to be blamed on the 'irresponsible' behaviour of the poor (notably the United States), and those states where 'structural explanations' are emphasised in interpreting the prevalence of poverty (particularly the Continental and Nordic countries in Europe) (Lepianka, Van Oorschot & Gelissen, 2009). The point to emphasise is that underlying public attitudes have implications for the viability and legitimacy of social policy programmes, as well as for the capacity of European social democratic parties to frame their agendas in terms of enduring social justice principles (Taylor-Gooby, 2012).

Attitudes are of course inherently complex: for example, findings from the most recent UK social attitudes survey show that public attitudes towards poverty and the poorest in society have hardened since the 1980s, despite the election of a Labour government committed to eradicating poverty. For example, in 1989, 51 per cent backed policies to redistribute income from rich to poor, but this had fallen to 36 per cent by 2015, although 78 per cent remain concerned about the extent of wealth inequality in the UK (Sage et al, 2015). Some commentators argue that the decline in support for policies to tackle poverty reflects the unwillingness of leading social democratic politicians in Britain to talk more explicitly about the case for redistribution and a comprehensive welfare state. However, political scientists have questioned this by proposing a so-called 'thermometer effect': voters will support a party which promises to correct current problems such as rising inequality, but once the party has entered power and enacted those policies, support for redistribution and higher taxes will inevitably decline.

Nonetheless, it is important to emphasise that while public perception helps to shape policymaking, governments have the power to influence perceptions in order to enhance the legitimacy of their policies. Political parties are not the passive beneficiaries of underlying shifts in public opinion, but rather have the capacity to frame and shape the attitudes and perceptions of voters. The centre ground of politics is not given, but can be contested and reshaped on the basis of a sharply defined ideological and programmatic appeal. Parties should actively seek to alter the public mood, rather than being imprisoned by a particular instinct as to what voters will, or will not, accept (Taylor-Gooby, 2013).

This concern with public attitudes has focused increasing attention on the processes of 'perception formation' among citizens, notably through the media. At the same time, it is important not to underestimate the importance of wider social influences and networks in shaping attitudes and values, as well as the role of ideas in framing public agendas. It is wrong to suppose that interests matter more than ideas, "since the interests which individuals pursue have to be articulated as ideas before they can be pursued as interests" (Gamble, 2009: 142). Ideas are more often weapons in the struggle to define the dominant discourse and conception of political 'common sense', shifting the axis of politics irreversibly in a social democratic direction. Unquestionably, ideas matter; there will be no revival of centre-left politics in Europe without a thoroughgoing and fundamental renewal of ideas.

PUBLIC ATTITUDES TO SOCIAL JUSTICE

How European social democratic parties and governments frame their appeal to social justice has major implications for their electoral salience and governing success. The various dimensions of social justice, to a greater or lesser extent, reflect intuitive understandings of fairness and desert, as such they help to ground centre-left politics in a broader conception of the common good. There are discernibly three key challenges ahead in developing the politics of social justice (Taylor-Gooby, 2013).

The first challenge concerns the importance of building 'reciprocity' in the welfare system. There is concern about the extent of income inequality, and broad support for redistribution from rich to poor. The needs of children are valued particularly highly, while able-bodied adults are expected to make a fair contribution, either through paid work in the labour market or by caring for dependants. There is strong evidence that European citizens favour 'participation' in socially valued activities, and are intolerant of 'freeriding' in the welfare state. This would suggest that the public will support measures that help people into work (such as free childcare and activation policies) which also address the adequacy of rewards (for example, measures to narrow the gender pay gap) (Mulgan, 2005).

The second point relates to the importance of public trust in governments and politicians. While citizens in most EU member states do lean towards support for redistribution, there is greater scepticism about whether national governments have the capacity to carry out redistribution fairly and legitimately. An issue that has been inflamed by the 2008 financial crisis concerns tax reform programmes which clamp down on evasion and non-payment of taxes. The evidence suggests that a convincing effort to penalise tax evasion and avoidance would do a great deal to restore public confidence in the capacities of the state. This also suggests that social democrats who rely on collective institutions to pursue their goals cannot afford to let government and politicians slide into public disrepute. Political trust is inextricably intertwined with the pursuit of social justice, and the centre left has to help improve the quality and transparency of public debate (Gamble, 2012).

The third challenge involves using political instruments to help reshape public attitudes and views. It is misguided merely to acquiesce to public opinion, engaging in a 'race to the bottom' on income and corporate tax rates; as Taylor-Gooby (2013) makes clear, this might actually serve to harden public attitudes in a negative direction. At the same time, centre-left parties have a responsibility to lead public attitudes, not merely to follow. There is nothing inexorable about trends in society such as individualisation and growing diversity invalidating social justice policies or destroying the basis for collective action. It is important that social democratic parties take responsibility and show that they can reframe public agendas.

All three key challenges are relevant to major debates in contemporary welfare policy, chiefly the future of universalism: a universal welfare state has been one of the core pillars of social justice in Europe since the second world war (Esping-Andersen, 1999).

In many European countries, centre-right governments have sought to question the viability of universalism in the wake of the global financial crisis; several arguments have been used to justify the cutting back of universal welfare (Horton & Gregory, 2009). The first argument is the need to reduce government deficits, and therefore to scale back welfare state coverage of major social programmes such as child benefit and universal pensions. The second is perhaps more principled, suggesting that universality involves transferring resources from the poor to the rich, and that targeting resources on the poorest is the best way to help those most in need. It is difficult to justify taxing those on low incomes merely to pay universal benefits to those on higher incomes (Horton & Gregory, 2009).

However, centre-left parties in Europe ought to be cautious about acquiescing to the ideological right's views about universalism and the welfare state. In fact, the more targeted welfare provision becomes, the less likely it is that services will be of the highest quality, as Richard Tittmuss famously predicted. Countries with higher degrees of targeting tend to be characterised by lower overall spending on the welfare state as a share of national income (Horton & Gregory, 2009). What such arguments disguise is a familiar ideological claim on the part of the right, namely that all forms of state provision create dependency, and that the purpose of government should be to keep spending and tax rates as low as possible.

This is diametrically at odds with social democratic principles: the welfare state was never chiefly concerned with charity or philanthropy, but with the idea of risk sharing and resource pooling: buying services and insurance through the state should encompass the entire population, not only the poor (Taylor-Gooby, 2012). At the same time, Nordic social democracy in particular has always seen welfare as integral to a sustainable model of capitalism: welfare is a source of wealth creation, not merely a drain on resources (Esping-Andersen, 2009). This encapsulates the basic synergy between economic efficiency and social justice: for example, ensuring that talented and highly skilled women can access the labour market entails universal, high-quality and affordable child care coverage for all families. This is a more substantive moral basis for the welfare state than the claim that those on higher incomes should support measures that reduce inequality which breeds social disorder and fragmentation. This claim was at the heart of *The Spirit Level* (Wilkinson & Pickett, 2009), but the argument underplays the extent to which universalism *directly* benefits the whole of society.

The defence of universalism is about protecting the long-term interests of the poorest in society, as well as reaching out to middle-class voters. A majoritarian welfare state can help to meet the aspirations of middle- and higher-income citizens, as well as preventing poverty among low-income households (Horton & Gregory, 2009). It is important to continue to challenge ideological arguments against universalism, engaging in a battle of ideas not only about the future of the welfare state, but the role of government in a rapidly changing world.

It is also imperative to make the case for universalism in today's society given the rise of new social risks, increasing wage and income inequality, and the desire for redistribution over the life-course (Taylor-Gooby, 2012). This can help to ease transitions, facilitating individual choices that enhance personal autonomy from caring to lifetime learning, a crucial dimension of social justice. While this chapter has not focused directly on the policy implications arising from these findings, it is worth reflecting on what public attitudes in Europe might say about how best to pursue the social justice agenda alongside welfare universalism:

- Social democrats have to be concerned not only with social justice, but economic dynamism. Support for effective strategies to counter poverty and inequality is strongest where there is confidence that economic growth will be sustained (Carlin, 2013). Social justice and economic dynamism can be reconciled, although it is important to be aware of potential trade-offs.
- Traditional redistributive mechanisms are necessary, but they may need to be modified in the light of structural change. For example, progressive taxation has an important role to play in redistributing

resources from rich to poor, but must not compromise economic needs or job creation (Aghion, 2014).

- While policy legitimately focuses on the needs of the long-term poor and excluded, it is important to be concerned with 'transitions', in particular the role of active labour markets in enabling people to escape poverty. There should be a strong emphasis on activating labour market strategies since active participation strengthens support for the welfare state (Esping-Andersen, 2009).

- Policies that are designed to help the poorest should also focus on in-work poverty, increasing financial support for carers and ensuring that an adequate structure for the minimum wage is in place across EU member states. Reducing child poverty must continue to have a central place in the social justice agenda of centre-left parties in Europe.

- Policies that benefit more affluent groups are important if they help to consolidate commitment to universalism in the welfare state.

- 'Gender-sensitive' policies are crucial, not only to continue improving the economic position of women, but also to provide greater support to parents and young families (Carlin, 2013). Exposing pay differentials between men and women will help to tackle the gender pay gap, backed by anti-discrimination legislation.

- The wealthy and high earners need to be properly incorporated within the obligations and duties of citizenship. Social responsibility must be exercised at the 'top' of society, not merely among the most excluded (Miller, 1994). The financial crisis appears to have opened up more space for radical action on pay and taxation.

- Finally, policy in nation states has to be matched by action at the EU level. 'Social Europe' has an important role to play, encouraging member states to benchmark progress on key indicators such as reducing child poverty; sharing best practice in solving the toughest challenges, notably long-term unemployment; and evolving new mechanisms such as the structural adjustment fund to mitigate the impact of social exclusion in the worst affected regions of the EU (Liddle & Lerais, 2006). Europe itself has to be a force for greater solidarity and social justice; the UK referendum on future membership of the EU demonstrated the negative consequences of failing to deal effectively with growing inequality and polarisation.

CONCLUSION

This chapter has argued that while there are inevitably a variety of ideas on which centre-left parties can draw, social democrats should focus on developing a new politics of social justice across Europe. It is essential to bring together an account of the various dimensions of social justice with an informed assessment of the underlying nature of public opinion. Recent research on poverty and inequality has tended to focus on underlying values, rather than examining what drives and motivates particular attitudes. Cross-national comparisons help to illuminate important underlying trends and patterns, while highlighting how particular issues and themes might be reframed in order to support social democratic objectives in an increasingly complex world. It is important to assess the underlying drivers of public opinion in order to build a new consensus for social justice in Europe. If social democrats articulate bold ideas that take account of intuitive public sentiments, they can reshape both institutions and interests, laying the ground for new majoritarian electoral coalitions. The answer, as the former SPD leader Willy Brandt once observed, is not to abandon traditional values but to 'dare more social democracy'.

Whatever ideas social democracy assembles at the national level, however, it needs to confront not only the growing challenge to nation states and the fundamental weakness of pursing a 'national road to socialism', but the growing counter-reaction to supranational politics, especially at the level of Europe. This dialectic between nation state politics and liberal internationalism is assessed in the next chapter.

NOTES

1. J.M. Keynes, *Essays in Persuasion*, London: 1931.

2. See Colin Crouch, *The Strange Non-Death of Neo-Liberalism*, Cambridge: Polity, 2011.

3. https://milescorak.com/2016/05/18/the-winners-and-losers-of-global-ization-branko-milanovics-new-book-on-inequality-answers-two-impor-tant-questions/

4. https://milescorak.com/2016/05/18/the-winners-and-losers-of-global-ization-branko-milanovics-new-book-on-inequality-answers-two-impor-tant-questions/

5. See R. Liddle & F. Lerais, 'Europe's Social Reality', Bureau of European Economic Advisers (BEPA), Brussels: European Commission, 2006.

6. David Miller, *Principles of Social Justice*, Cambridge, Mass: Harvard University Press, 1994.

HOW DOES THE CENTRE LEFT RESPOND? SOCIAL JUSTICE IN THE 'NEW HARD TIMES'

The argument of this book is that centre-left parties need an electoral strategy and a governing strategy if they are to achieve political success. Despite many obstacles and challenges ahead, social democratic parties have the opportunity to fashion a new centre-left era centred on progressive ideas. In recent decades, centre-left parties have performed relatively poorly, and the politics of Europe and the United States are seen to be increasingly dominated by the populism of left and right. There is nothing inevitable about social change, nor do the majority of voters necessarily want to be governed by populist parties: most voters want stable, competent and broadly progressive government. Social democrats should have confidence despite the unpropitious nature of the political environment in which they operate.

The aim of an electoral strategy is to build new coalitions across society, forging cross-class social and political alliances. There is an argument within social democratic parties about whether the left should uniquely represent the working class, but in every country, the left can only achieve power and be in government where it secures the votes of the broader middle and working class. This has been the case for half a century: centre-left parties have to represent and govern for the whole nation. In the early 20th century, revisionist pioneers such as Eduard Bernstein, Jean Jaurès and Keir Hardie insisted that socialism meant a war against a system rather than a class. The only means by which social reforms could be enacted was through class cooperation forging a common purpose, rather than class conflict and the politics of confrontation.

Of course, centre-left parties are operating in an environment where the politics of identity increasingly trump the politics of class. As already discussed in this book, they need an electoral strategy that is able to reconcile the 'materialist' concerns of the working class and aspirant middle, who focus on wages and income distribution, with the 'non-materialist' values of the middle class who are concerned with the environment, quality of life, and individual rights. They have to reconcile the interests and values of those who fear economic change and openness with those who embrace global economic integration. This means tapping into the potential for new class alliances across society: for example, Anne Wren (2013) has strongly emphasised the need for centre-left parties to embrace high-income working women and parents who favour state intervention and regulation to make the economy fit for working families.

Having won elections, the centre left's governing strategy should be built on two central pillars: radical policy innovation that rebuilds economic credibility and trust, alongside the new politics of identity. In an era of constrained national budgets and lower economic growth, social democrats will have to deliver services and benefits in new ways, while retaining their core economic competence. At the same time, they need to anchor centre-left politics in a coherent conception of national identity in a Europe where national, regional and local identities are being reasserted. Social democrats must show that citizens do not have to choose between a strong regional identity, a strong national identity, and a strong European identity. Nor is the sovereignty of states ever 'zero sum': the capacity of governments and public institutions to regulate the economy, for example, can be strengthened at regional, national *and* European level. There are some who argue that Europeanisation has denuded centre-left political parties of the capacity to exercise leverage over the economy due to the 'shackles' imposed by membership of European Monetary Union (EMU). This perspective fails to appreciate how the capacity of governments to act has been rebuilt at both national and European level.

POLICY INNOVATION AND ECONOMIC TRUST

In an era of relative economic stagnation, it is necessary to identify new routes to social justice where the left cannot rely on continuous rises in public spending: the new realities are lower economic growth; the pressures of demographic change and an ageing society; and the fact that old-style spending and benefits do not always effectively address intractable problems such as worklessness and family instability means that traditional approaches must be re-thought (Taylor-Gooby, 2013). In recent decades it has increasingly been recognised that social policy on its own cannot make society more equal. The left has to identify more sustainable and egalitarian models of capitalism; social justice is easier to achieve in countries where the economic system is likely to achieve greater equality in the distribution of primary incomes.

PREDISTRIBUTIVE REFORM STRATEGIES

In the light of these challenges, progressives need to advocate bold reforms built around a 'predistributive' strategy to promote middle-class families, while tilting the balance of structural advantage towards those from low- and middle-income households. Jacob Hacker has described predistribution as about "making markets work for the middle class". This deviates from earlier third way thinking since predistribution acknowledges that markets left to their own devices will not deliver socially efficient or just outcomes; the third way failed to provide a positive account of the state's role in regulating a complex and structurally unstable globalised economy; and the traditional strategy of redistribution puts centre-left parties in an untenable position, since a growing chorus of complaint about 'freeriding' and 'undeserving' groups dependent on welfare provision erodes support for government redistribution over time.

The locus of predistribution is rebuilding support for collective security and public service provision, reducing structural dependency on the state, while tackling the underlying causes of wage and income inequality instead of relying on *post hoc* redistribution. The predistributive strategy starts from the need to develop countervailing powers to shape the outcomes of markets, rather than leaving markets free to operate without oversight or intervention. Policy reforms include:

- *Macroeconomic reform to correct sectoral and distributional balances.* Aggressive monetary policy intervention such as quantitative easing helped to prevent the 2008–9 crisis turning from a recession into a depression, but the long-term impact has been a major redistribution in favour of the top five per cent: the 'asset-earning classes'. Those who depend on wages and interest on savings in retirement have been hardest hit. The strategy of nominal inflation targeting in central banks, including in the European Central Bank, has to be revisited to prioritise full employment and growth, especially in southern Europe (Carlin, 2013).
- *Tax reforms to make taxation regimes more progressive.* Policymakers must focus their attention on assets such as property, and unearned income such as inheritance, which are more immobile and therefore harder to evade. Taxation systems are more likely to be progressive if a system of tax credits is adopted, rather than raising tax thresholds, which tends to benefit higher-income earners. Tax credits can be used to support the incomes and childcare costs of relatively hard-pressed middle-class families, rather than just the lowest earners in making work pay (Horton & Gregory, 2009).
- *A revamped education and skills strategy to address the technology and automation challenge.* All governments since the 1990s have paid lip service to the importance of 'lifetime learning'. Now, more than ever, it is a necessity as workers have to adapt

to new technologies throughout their working lives. A personal learning account where individuals can invest in their own human capital as well as further and higher education – with incentives from the state through tax breaks and subsidised loans – would generate a new culture of active education and learning 'from the cradle to the grave'. Equally vital is to protect investment in early years intervention and education, the best approach to narrowing cognitive gaps between children from low- and high-income households.

- *Measures to democratise human capital and asset ownership.* The 'jobs for wages model' is under pressure as technological change and the global labour force weaken the bargaining position of middle-class as well as low-skilled workers. If more groups are to share in the fruits of rising prosperity, the distribution of assets and the spread of ownership will need to be significantly expanded. Three areas are especially important. First, widening the base of employee share ownership and profit sharing. Second, expanding the pool of home owners, not by encouraging reckless lending to vulnerable households, but through a major extension of 'part-rent, part-buy' schemes through which an asset stake can be accumulated gradually over time, combined with major capital investment in housing infrastructure. Finally, fashioning an EU-wide 'baby bond': an asset stake to which every child would be entitled through a combination of government contribution and parental saving, addressing the distribution of assets as well as incomes.
- *Measures to make the labour market fairer by developing countervailing pressures to economic forces that accentuate polarisation and inequality.* Liberal market economies in particular have promoted the goal of employment creation, but at the expense of rising wage inequalities for which the state needs to make increasingly costly compensation. More effective protection not only includes statutory minimum wages and sectoral intervention in low-wage sectors, but encouraging collective agreements through trade unions, employee representative organisations, and social networks to organise workers in low-skilled sectors, strengthening their

capacity to negotiate pay bargaining arrangements. The Nordic states have shown how structured approaches to wage negotiation are consistent with open, globalised economies (Callaghan, 2009).

- *Expanding service sector jobs in caring sectors to widen employment opportunity.* This approach requires de-industrialised countries to rebuild their traded and export-led sectors through policies designed to promote innovation and growth, using the fruits of higher GDP to provide high quality public services while offering opportunities for the less productive majority of workers in the 'non-traded' services sector (Carlin, 2013). This is where most jobs for the low to middle skilled in the industrialised economies will be created, assisting middle-class families by ensuring a supply of high quality caring services. Another challenge relates to expanding productivity in these sectors though new technologies and investing in the up-skilling of the workforce (Carlin, 2013).

- *Structural reforms to improve the quality of public services.* A key pillar of middle-class security is the ability of families to access high quality services such as health and education which the market cannot be relied upon to provide. As real incomes rise over generations, citizens naturally come to have higher expectations of public services, and are willing to invest additional disposable income via taxes or alternatively, through private provision where their aspirations are not being satisfied. Moreover, technological change, demography and ageing are imposing new cost pressures on healthcare and education systems. In an era of constrained resources, it is vital that structural reforms can be implemented to make services more effective and cost efficient. This goes beyond introducing private providers and the outsourcing of provision, the 'new public management' obsession of the 1990s. It is about creating 'whole systems' of integrated provision which manage and contain demand in public services, preventing problems at the outset rather than treating symptoms, harnessing public, non-state and private actors to upgrade collective services.

- *Championing gender equality remains the key to rebuilding support for inclusive and broad-based social security.* Most industrialised countries over the last three decades have witnessed the rapid entry of women into the labour force, but this remains an 'unfinished revolution' (Esping-Andersen, 2009). Women appear to have a comparative advantage in high-skilled service sector occupations, while the evidence is that women in employment are significantly more likely to support welfare policies such as universal childcare, adequate elderly care, shared parental leave, public employment and collective provision (Wren, 2013). These policies must be combined with measures to reduce employment and pay discrimination in labour markets, eroding the 'motherhood pay penalty' that many working women still face.
- *Finally, investing in infrastructure and SME formation as a spur to growth.* Social democrats need a strategy for dynamic production and wealth creation, not only fairer distribution. The best way to support middle-class incomes and living standards is to ensure sustainable growth, which leads to rising nominal wages and an expanded tax base that can be reinvested in caring services for families. Boosting growth in Europe requires structural reforms, not the short-term fixes of public and private debt financing. That includes improving access to finance for SMEs and mid-caps, promoting hi-tech manufacturing through investment in research and development, and strengthening the role of the higher education sector in technology and innovation diffusion (Aghion, 2014). An enlarged European Infrastructure Bank will help to modernise and upgrade member states' long-term productive capabilities.

All of these measures will need to be implemented through effective European institutions which ensure not only recovery and resilience after the financial crisis, but long-term growth, improvements in social wellbeing, and ecological sustainability. A strategy of pursuing inclusive, pro-growth policies 'in one country' is untenable:

there has to be coordinated international action and cross-national benchmarking led by a strong EU among a diversity of nation states.

Moreover, while structural forces are putting unprecedented pressures and strains on existing socioeconomic models, this is not a simplistic story of societal polarisation. The wealthy few enjoy unprecedented rewards and the most excluded groups continue to suffer adverse life chances; but it is the broad middle class which more than ever feels the spread of insecurity as incomes are squeezed. Social democracy has to stand up for the struggling middle class if it is to help those most in need: to maintain consent for universal social security; to generate the growth needed for investment in public goods; and to ensure a dynamic economy and society. As the Swedish social democratic leader Olof Palme once declared, 'secure people dare'.

One further opportunity for the left is decentralisation and learning from localised experiments; centre-left parties are often successful at local government and mayoral level; they should use this strength to develop national policy strategies; this can be augmented by benchmarking and policy learning at the EU level. Above all, there is an acute need for rigour about collecting and applying evidence: policy programmes that do not achieve results weaken confidence in active government.

A credible centre-left governing strategy should focus resolutely on boosting the education, skills and human capital of the entire population, especially the most disadvantaged. The key insight for policymakers is that what occurs outside formal institutions through the home environment, with parents, and among peers is as significant as what takes place in schools and learning institutions. The priority should be policies that equalise opportunities in an era where there is a widening gulf between young people born into economic advantage, and those who are not. In that context, the following policy measures have been proposed in the UK at the national and local level:

- *Refocus early intervention strategies.* Additional interventions in the early years have been a priority for policymakers across the political spectrum, although investment in Sure Start has been cut back since 2010–11. The previous Labour administration invested heavily in nursery provision, but the early years never received the concerted attention given to schools and the NHS. Childcare is more expensive in the UK than most comparable economies; there are growing concerns about the adequacy of coverage, 'post-code lotteries', and lower quality. As a consequence, the UK has a relatively low rate of female employment, ranking 15th in the OECD. There are two crucial aspects of policy that should not be allowed to slip off the agenda. The first is to ensure that resources and infrastructure are weighted towards the most disadvantaged groups within a universal model. Second, at its inception Sure Start was strongly orientated towards parental involvement, not only in the settings themselves, but in the management and governance of Sure Start centres. This dimension of parental empowerment has been weakened, and ought to be re-activated.

- *Boost parenting support.* In a challenging economic environment with a host of pervasive social stress factors, parents need effective support. Mentoring has proven beneficial effects, where more experienced parents support those facing difficulties. Formal parenting programmes can be useful, but often more informal support built around Sure Start, early years provision, and schools and youth centres is necessary. Initiatives such as Nurse-Family Partnerships, where nurses support parents in disadvantaged households from the prenatal stage through to early childhood, are crucial too.
- *Improve the quality of parenting.* There is an extensive public policy literature on the potential of behavioural change strategies to improve outcomes. How parents interact with their children can have a significant impact on later achievement. For example, parents who regularly read to their children significantly improve their cognitive outcomes; responding appropriately to misbehaviour can also help to prevent later conduct disorders (Dearden et al., 2009). It is important to remember that parenting is not always provided by biological parents, but a range of care-givers, including grandparents and family friends.

- *Encourage parental responsibilities.* Parents have the right to support and to be able to access state-funded services, but parents also have reciprocal obligations including ensuring good school attendance and behaviour. Where responsibilities are breached, mechanisms such as 'home-school contracts' and 'parenting orders' might be necessary to ensure that the underlying causes of negative behaviour are addressed.
- *Extend the 'pupil premium' and reform the system of school choice.* The pupil premium in England has provided schools who accept pupils from disadvantaged households with an additional £950 per child in 2015–16. Nonetheless, the evidence is that children from low-income households continue to access the most poorly performing schools (Allen & Burgess, 2011). This needs to be addressed by boosting the premium available for pupils from disadvantaged backgrounds, while opening up the school selection process to avoid residential segregation. At the same time, highly performing schools need additional incentives to expand.
- *Promote multi-agency working across public services.* Improving the situation facing the most disadvantaged children and young people requires not only input from schools and Sure Start centres, but all public services locally and nationally. The impact of health inequalities on human capital acquisition and relative social mobility, for example, is now well documented. In New York, a hub 'children's zone' model has been used to provide intensive support to disadvantaged families in low-income neighbourhoods.

Indeed, expanding social investment to focus on pupils from low income households will reap long-term rewards. For example, the Institute for Public Policy Research (IPPR) estimates that universal, affordable childcare will boost the female employment rate and government tax revenues: an initial, up-front investment achieves average returns of £20,050 over four years. Future governments will, nevertheless, have to demonstrate how this is to be paid for. IPPR propose to rationalise tax credits and childcare subsidies into increased supply-side funding for early years' provision. Alternative options include rationalising benefits to relatively well-off pension-ers such as free travel and the winter fuel allowance, as well as taxing capital, property, wealth and inheritance more efficiently: for example, a lifetime gifts tax could raise £1bn; abolishing higher-rate tax relief on pensions would generate a further £7bn; a property-based 'mansion tax' could raise a further £3bn for the UK exchequer (Taylor-Gooby, 2013).

Raising the burden of taxation is never popular, but two principles ought to be enunciated in the debate. First, additional 'wealth' taxes ought to be 'hypothecated': pooled into a specific fund designed to offset adverse 'social inheritance', boosting opportunities for those from disadvantaged backgrounds. Second, the better-off older generations acknowledge that younger people and families increas-ingly need support: modest tax rises and benefit rationalisation is necessary to ensure intergenerational reciprocity. Early intervention, family support and education are not a solution to every social and economic problem. Nonetheless, it is difficult to imagine that rising inequality and lower earnings mobility can be countered without more effective intervention that boosts the relative position of chil-dren and young people from low-income households. Until recently, this dimension has been missing from much of the literature on 'predistribution'; it is essential to integrate the social investment approach into future strategies designed to improve predistributive outcomes in the UK and beyond.

ECONOMIC POLICY AFTER THE CRISIS: TOWARDS A NEW POLITICS OF PRODUCTION

The foundation of any viable policy agenda will be sustained and continuous economic growth. The left in Europe has to identify a new politics of production and growth in the wake of the crisis. The growth situation in the eurozone underlines the catastrophic damage and continuing aftershocks inflicted by the financial melt-down in 2008–9, exacerbated by the neverending euro crisis.

Despite its disastrous track record of macroeconomic management, epitomised by the Lawson boom in the late 1980s and George Osborne's ill-timed retrenchment after 2010, the Conservatives in Britain like other Christian democratic parties in western Europe have positioned themselves as the parties of fiscal discipline and economic competence, as well as the parties of entrepreneurship and material affluence. By contrast, for decades the left was seen as interested in fair distribution, while oblivious to expanding the frontiers of production. Harold Wilson's 'White Heat of Technology' in 1964 and Tony Blair's 'New Britain' in 1997 were exceptions to the rule. British Labour strove to secure a fairer share of the cake on behalf of the organised working class, whereas the Conservatives claimed to be able to grow the cake and spread the benefits among all classes and interests in society.

The principal task for parties of the left is to secure the mantle of fiscal credibility recognising that much of the credibility so painstakingly established after 1992 has been lost. This need not entail simply mimicking the right's programme of cuts. What is required is discipline in managing the public finances, with a root and branch review of all current expenditure. The UK economy was among the most indebted in the OECD, second only to Japan in total levels of public sector, financial, and household debt (Gamble, 2012). Nonetheless, the challenge for the left is more profound than merely rebuilding confidence in its economic management credentials; the key is framing a credible, post-crisis growth strategy, a new politics of production for our economies.

The seismic impact of the crisis has underlined the need for fresh thinking and ideas. Previous crises have been accompanied by radical questioning of existing political and economic orthodoxies. Since 2008–9, however, most political debate has focused on restoring the economy to 'business as usual': although the power of government was used to stabilise the financial system through bailouts and nationalisations, in stark contrast to the 1930s New Deal era there is no obvious enthusiasm for entrusting the state with new powers and responsibilities (Gamble, 2012). What is clear is that a radical programme for British and continental European social democracy is unlikely to emerge from 'ivory tower' blueprints. It is more likely to be forged through a process of 'bold, persistent experimentation', in Franklin Delano Roosevelt's memorable phrase.

Whatever reforms are undertaken to avert catastrophe in the eurozone, it is clear that sustainable, long-term growth will only be possible if there is a systemic shift of wealth and power within the global system (Strange, 1997). This requires some form of global polity rather than the fragmented structure of nation states. Despite the deep disconnect between European elites and citizens, the EU is an association of constitutional, democratic states that has numerous advantages (Gamble, 2012). Recognising that all countries remain part of an interdependent European and global economy, able to influence and shape the international system, will be essential for future prosperity and growth. Parties of the left succeed when they embrace the future instead of rehashing the debates and achievements of the past. Elections are not about seeking the gratitude of the voters; they are about vision and change. The left has to demonstrate it understands the forces and trends that are remaking our societies from globalisation to individualisation, demography and ageing.

A NEW POLITICS OF NATIONAL IDENTITY

Nonetheless, social democracy cannot rely on economic credibility and policy innovation alone; voters do not just want better political management: they want politicians who recognise their need for identity and a sense of belonging. Historically, social democracy as a political movement was firmly attached to the nation state (Berman, 2006); in the first world war, social democratic parties divided along national lines with the exception of individual leaders like Keir Hardie and Eduard Bernstein. This set the frame for the next century: in an era where national identities have solidified and the nation state has been re-asserted, social democrats have to embrace national identity but argue it is by no means inconsistent with political action at the European level.

Rather than merely devising a new policy programme, it is necessary to address a deeper question about the relationship between social democracy, national identity, and the nation state. Social democracy historically sought to move beyond the predominantly national sphere (Sassoon, 1996). Indeed, the roots of social democracy were internationalist: early social democratic parties and movements saw themselves as acting outside existing forms of the state, which were associated with the privileged order of the ancien regime; a fundamental tenet of early conceptions of socialism and social democracy inherited from Karl Marx and Friedrich Engels was that "the working class had no country" (Gamble, 2009). The new world order that socialism wished to bring about had the potential to transcend national divisions.

After the first world war, social democracy became largely national in character; the impact of the war was to reinforce national identity alongside feelings of belonging and chauvinism, both among both the working class and the ruling class of western Europe (Sassoon, 1996). The collapse of the liberal economic order that culminated in the great depression of the 1930s reinforced the tendency to look towards the nation state as the engine of economic and political reform; after 1945, national social democracy was in the ascendancy (Gamble, 2009). The macroeconomic regime of planning, national regulation and public ownership underpinned by the Keynesian welfare state offset the pressures in a capitalist economy towards greater inequality and instability; social democratic regimes throughout western Europe were able to shape markets in the public interest using the levers of the nation state to redistribute and regulate the economy, as Andrew Gamble has attested.

Of course, the notion that there has ever been a pure form of social democracy in one country is questionable; historically, states have long been interdependent and intertwined (Sorenson, 2004). No state throughout history has ever been entirely free of international pressures and obligations, as evidenced by debates stretching back to the 15th and 16th centuries about the role of national currencies and the relative merits of free trade, mercantilism and national protectionism

(Gamble, 2009). Since the 1970s, the impact of global forces has appeared to grow as the result of the globalisation of production, the creation of a global labour market, and the increase in migration that erodes the standards and citizenship benefits achieved in particular national economies (Albrow, 1996).

The contemporary dilemma facing all centre-left parties is that for most of the last century social democracy was national in its formation and preoccupations (Strange, 1996). The strategies developed by social democrats for pursuing economic growth, social justice and the public good were focused on the nation state and national governments (Gamble, 2009). This reached its height between the 1940s and the 1970s when it was believed that the economy, society and culture would be modernised through state intervention. Sovereignty was judged to reside within the boundaries of the nation state, overseen by national political elites accountable to citizens through periodic democratic elections (Sassoon, 1996).

One telling criticism made of centre-left parties in the 1980s and 1990s is that they were pursuing a strategy of 'social democracy in one country', namely 'the national road to socialism' (Callaghan, 2009). This approach was pursued initially by François Mitterrand's Socialist government in France, but it had resonance across western Europe, including in Britain. Over time, social democrats shifted their position, marked by growing acceptance of the case for European integration. In the UK, the vision of a more 'social Europe' contrasted starkly with the structural reforms of the economy and labour markets being enacted by the Thatcher governments. In the late 1980s social democrats embraced the European project, drawing on an internationalist tradition within social democratic parties.

The centre left has to come to terms with the limits of 'social democracy in one country' given the context of globalisation and liberalisation in the world economy. More recently, 'Europeanisation' and 'nationalism' have been counter posed as competing alternatives. However, there are critics on both sides who argue that the erosion of nation state capacity has been exaggerated (Sorenson, 2004).

There are other commentators who suggest that reconstituting the nation state remains a core challenge for social democratic politics.

In considering the future of liberal democracy and the fate of contemporary politics, social democrats must address the internationalisation of society and the economy without conceding the retreat of the nation state. As Gamble has argued, *national* social democracy is the platform on which a *European* and *global* social democracy will be built. This should not imply that transnational social democracy ought merely to replicate national social democracy: many institutions and ideas at the international level will have to be different. (Gamble, 2009)

For global governance and international social democracy to be viable, national politics and the nation state have to be strengthened. The weakness of much of the academic literature on globalisation is the implication that increasing the capacity of the global polity has to mean weakening the role of the nation state. It is mistaken to abandon national political action in favour of global political action, as theorists such as Martin Albrow (1996) and Susan Strange (1996) have acknowledged. The vibrancy of the global polity is dependent on embedding norms of democratic participation and accountability at the national level (Gamble, 2009). However, these democratic norms are under growing challenge in much of the industrialised world.

Social democrats have to strengthen the interventionist and developmental capacities of national governments, while encouraging the growth of global political institutions that can help to steer and reshape globalisation (Sorenson, 2004). These are two sides of the same coin: a global polity will not be created if national politics remains weak and fragmented (Gamble, 2009). At the same time, national governments will struggle to produce meaningful solutions without the capacity to act on a European and international scale: it is highly unlikely that key social democratic principles such as social justice can be advanced and entrenched unless collective action is possible both at the national and international level (Sapir, 2014).

The development of the global polity requires the embedding of the norms of constitutional government: unfettered, unaccountable political and economic power has to be constrained through effective regulation at the national and global level (Gamble, 2012). Many actors, particularly multinational and global corporations, have been able to exercise power without substantive accountability or scrutiny. In particular, they have been able to negotiate preferential arrangements with national governments on tax and regulation so as to undermine citizens' confidence in the tax state with negative implications for social democracy (Streek, 2014). At the same time, national democracies are under increasing strain, and are less able than ever to meet the challenges of being representative, responsible, and participative (Gamble, 2009). Citizen disengagement is widespread and is growing with many different manifestations and consequences; one particular irony is that power imbalances and lack of accountability at the global level are projected on to dissatisfaction with national democracies and national governments (Albrow, 1996). The key political challenges that need to be addressed in relation to representative democracy and the national polity according to Gamble are as follows:

- First, citizen disengagement from the political system and falling electoral turnouts is creating a crisis of representation in western industrialised societies;
- Second, the apparent weakening of accountability and general disillusionment with the public sector is leading to diminishing faith in what governments can deliver for citizens;
- Third, the growth of expertise, technocratic management and the 'depoliticisation' of sensitive policy issues may threaten participative democracy and undermine political debate (Gamble, 2009: 67).

This points towards the need for more effective systems of global governance, not only national political reform. But social democrats cannot think in more transnational and cosmopolitan terms in the global polity without engaging with problems that currently afflict national social democracy, in particular citizen disengagement, loss of accountability, and the rise of complexity and depoliticisation (Gamble, 2009). The crisis of trust, legitimacy and accountability cannot be solved by turning away from domestic politics; however, national politics will not be strengthened merely by undermining European or global institutions (Stoker, 2006). The interdependent nature of the domestic and international arenas has to be understood. The following section addresses each of the key challenges in turn.

Citizen disengagement

The declining participation of citizens in electoral politics is a long-term development evidenced by decreasing turnout in local, national and European elections. The trends in the UK, continental Europe and the United States are reviewed in Gerry Stoker's survey of modern democracy, *Why Politics Matters?* (2006). The claim is that despite the increasing availability of information and knowledge in western societies alongside rising levels of education, fewer voters seem engaged in formal political institutions centred on traditional parties and electoral competition. The ideological nature of politics in the aftermath of the second world war has been displaced by a form of political deliberation that is increasingly about brand, style and personality, further exacerbated by the trivialised media reporting of politics. The media now acts as the major intermediary between voters, politicians and national governments, but often appears to encourage apathy and disillusionment (Stoker, 2006).

The arguments for the decline of democratic institutions and democratic politics are wide-ranging and ought not to be over-stated. There are trends and counter-trends in the data; it is wrong to imply that national politics has become denuded of serious debate and ideological choice. Nonetheless, it seems undeniable that the class basis of social democracy as a struggle for social justice within the nation state on behalf of the manual working class is much weaker than it was. There is evidence that centre-left parties no longer play such an important role in mobilising low income and economically marginalised households to participate in the electoral process (Curtice, Heath & Jowell, 2005).

Accountability and sovereignty

The second claim is that the capacity of national governments to deliver positive outcomes for citizens has been curtailed since the 1970s: the fragmentation of the public sector and the traditional state appears to make governments less able to influence society (Sorenson, 2004). Power has passed 'upwards' towards the European Union and global political institutions, 'sideways' to global corporations and the private sector, and 'downwards' to the multiple actors within civil society from NGOs to the voluntary sector (Guy-Peters, 2004). What has apparently emerged is the era of "the stateless state" (Bevir & Rhodes, 2005).

Moreover, national political elites can barely resist the temptation to put the blame for unpopular decisions onto other tiers of the state, which fuels cynicism about representative democracy and the system of government. The European Union has often been the target; but national politicians have failed to register that undermining the European project merely amplifies disillusionment with all forms of collective politics, including national politics and national governments (Gamble, 2009).

At the same time, in a multilateral world where policy is increasingly negotiated in a transnational political space, it can be difficult for citizens to understand where decisions are made and in whose interests (Guy-Peters, 2004). Institutions such as the European commission, the European Court of Justice, and the World Trade Organisation seemingly constrain what national politicians can do. There are unrealistic expectations about the capacity and competence of governments to deliver outcomes favoured by citizens, which politicians have often done little to constrain and have even encouraged (White, 1999). On entering government, elected ministers too often find that they do not have the levers to achieve what they promised during the campaign, fuelling the resentment and mistrust of voters.

It is mistaken to argue that governments have lost the capacity to intervene and regulate the economy, or to 'modernise' state and society (Mulgan, 2005). What they need is to reconstitute their capabilities in the light of economic fragmentation, the globalisation of the world economy, and deep social change (Guy-Peters, 2004). At the same time, it is clear that markets, civil society and public institutions cannot be easily controlled and steered by national governments, nor should they be. Social democracy should abandon its long-held obsession with to top-down 'mechanical' control.

Complexity and knowledge

The final challenge relates to complexity and depoliticisation, where key policy decisions are allegedly taken out of the process of democratic deliberation. This has encouraged the development of managerial and technocratic politics both nationally and globally, over which citizens often appear to have little influence. National governments have struggled to manage the consequences of technological change and scientific development, which requires increasing dependence on specialist expertise (Gamble, 2009). On issues such as climate change, energy, GM foods, genetic selection, and the invention of pharmaceuticals and drugs, governments rely on the insight of experts; but scientists themselves often disagree about the causes and consequences of problems (Sorenson, 2004). Evaluation evidence in public policy is rarely straightforward. The implications for political decision-making are not necessarily clearcut: this ambiguity and uncertainty leaves anxious voters even more concerned and confused.

The response of many governments has been to 'depoliticise' key decisions, setting up 'arms-length' boards of experts to take decisions on their behalf, removing ministers from the decision-making process and making political elites less accountable for errors that occur (Stoker, 2006). Yet inevitably politicians get the blame when things go wrong, as it is often difficult to distinguish between political accountability and operational responsibility. The effect of depoliticisation has been to pull citizens and politicians even further apart, creating the impression that there are few ideological choices left, and that many outcomes are inevitable (Gamble, 2009). Rather than complex trade-offs, there are apparently inevitable forces which cannot be resisted, hence the language of 'no alternative' at the core of neoliberalism. Nothing could do more to alienate citizens from the arenas of democratic politics and deliberation.

It ought to be remembered that political systems are highly resilient and ever changing. The issues referred to in this book offer a multitude of opportunities to strengthen national and global politics, rather than threatening the 'end of western democracy'. There are many trends and counter-trends; it is mistaken to extrapolate from a relatively brief period of historical change. The doomsayers who predict the erosion and atrophy of civil society have overstated their case (Stoker, 2006).

Nonetheless, there are serious issues and problems to be confronted. Social democrats in particular have much to lose if the corrosive loss of faith in politics is not addressed: collective solutions to society's problems are only possible through effective and accountable democratic institutions. National social democracy is the institutional platform on which a vibrant and accountable European and global polity will be built (Runciman, 2013). Above all, social democrats must fight to retain the sense of politics as an open process in which there are real choices to be made that are not foreordained (Gamble, 2009). Citizens can shape the destiny of their societies, rather than being the victims of circumstances beyond their collective control.

SOCIAL DEMOCRACY AND THE NATION STATE

In the light of these developments, social democrats have to recast their view of the state. After the financial crisis, active government intervention regained legitimacy in order to stabilise the banking system, support the wider economy, and protect citizens from global economic storms. It was far from clear, however, that the state was back as a major actor in the context of an internationalised economy. In part, citizens were still concerned about the encroachment of centralised bureaucracy, and its damaging effect on innovation and growth. Relatively high levels of public sector debt and greater scepticism about higher taxes given the tight squeeze on the wages and incomes of the struggling middle class further depleted support for the extended state. At the same time, globalisation continued to erode the 'steering capacities' of the nation state. As a result, the role of the state is still politically contested on left and right.

The assumption that the goal of social democracy is to win power over the central state, using the state to reshape society and the economy, still influences many conceptions of centre-left politics; nevertheless, it has never been tenable even in the era of mass industrialisation. In contemporary society, it implies a relationship between citizen and state in which expectations are encouraged that cannot realistically be met, leading to often violent swings, "between unrealistic hope and unfounded disillusionment" (Gamble, 2009: 74).

Achieving formal political power, of course, remains an important objective for all social democratic parties. What is needed is a vision of politics that is able to face up to intractable dilemmas and trade-offs, acknowledging the complexity of problems in a way that engages citizens (Gamble, 2012).

In the future, parties that are both electorally and politically successful will be capable of seizing the agenda, promoting institutional innovation and renewal. This will occur against the backdrop of unprecedented shocks to the global economy, changes in the nature of social citizenship, and threats to the survival of the planet. It will demand a new relationship between state and citizen, neither the laissez-faire ethos of the 1980s nor the paternalism of the 1940s. It will mean ceasing to conflate collective action with state power, finding alternative approaches to promoting the public interest and delivering public goods. Social democrats will need to rediscover a set of governing principles that seek to do things with people, not to them: that recognises citizens want to be the agents of political change for themselves.

The politics of democratic engagement and solidarity building is vital to the future centre left. Deepening democracy through an extension of proportional representation in electoral systems to ensure that the vote of every citizen counts equally is fundamental. Protecting citizens from arbitrary abuse by either the state or the private and corporate sector is an imperative. Governments have to be responsive and accountable, rather than encouraging a 'take-it-or-leave-it' culture. There is a vibrant inheritance of ideologies, institutions and ideas on which the centre left can draw (Gamble, 2010). This lineage includes the civic republican tradition which emphasises the autonomy of citizens, and the imperative of devolving and diffusing power as widely as possible.

CONCLUSION

Giving citizens and communities the control and responsibility to govern their own lives, as well as breaking with the commitment to centralised government, ought to be a key test of the social democratic 'good society'. The centre left has for decades focused on top-down reforms of the market and the state, paying too little attention to how mobilising civil society can achieve social democratic goals. Traditionally the debate on the left was between revisionists who favoured the 'parliamentary road' to social democracy, and socialists who believed this strategy would inevitably fail: the left needed to devise an 'extra-parliamentary' model of political change embracing social activism and movement politics. In truth, this was always a false choice: many social and economic reforms can only be achieved through the democratic process, but the likelihood of doing so depends on the political energy unleashed by civil society. Many centre-left aims can be realised through social networks and civic activism outside the formal arena of legislation and regulation. Nevertheless, bottom-up action will have greater efficacy if there is a model of political economy which recognises the importance of social inclusion and environmental sustainability. The aim of social democracy is still the long-term transformation of society as it was in the era of Eduard Bernstein and Karl Kautsky at the dawn of the 20th century.

CONCLUSION

The crisis and 'retreat' of European social democracy

"The decadent international but individualistic capitalism in the hands of which we found ourselves ... is not a success. It is not intelligent. It is not beautiful. It is not just. It is not virtuous. And it doesn't deliver the goods."

J.M. Keynes[1]

To chart a way back to government for the centre left, social democracy needs a strategy to connect the politics of support with the politics of power: there is little purpose in winning elections unless there is a coherent strategy for how to govern afterwards. Across Europe and the US, the priority for progressives remains to build a more productive and innovative model of capitalism: leading the world in innovation; generating more secure, well-paid jobs; and rebalancing the distribution of rewards towards those on low and middle incomes.

Social democracy has to regain its reputation for economic competence, while reclaiming the politics of national identity to make the case for liberal internationalism and a strong Europe. As the political scientist Sheri Berman (2006) has noted, centre-left parties in western Europe have traditionally enjoyed an uneasy relationship with nationalism. Karl Marx envisaged a world where 'all workers would unite' across national borders; but Berman observes

that centre-left parties had to strike a compromise with nationalism to gain electoral strength in the early 20th century. For social
democracy to offer hope, its core political identity and governing
strategy has to be recast for the 'new hard times' through which we
are living. The centre left has to identify a new raison d'être for the
post-crisis age, developing a fairer, more inclusive capitalism as the
foundation of a more equal society. This is an agenda for nation
states working in conjunction with a more effective and representative EU. Yes, citizens need to feel a sense of national belonging and
identity, but cooperation between states will be vital in the future.
Any permanent lapse into nationalism and protectionism will have
detrimental effects on our economies and societies.

Why is this agenda not the third-way approach of the 1990s? At the
policy level, it is more critical of capitalism and the market; it recognises the tension between nationhood and the European polity; it advo-
cates radical reform of democracy and the state. At the political level,
the new social democratic agenda acknowledges that centre-left parties have to narrow the gap between their traditional supporters and the
'post-materialist' middle class; social democracy has to build bridges
between those who favour economic change and openness, and those
groups who resist structural change. As Dani Rodrik suggests:

> A crucial difference between the right and the left is that the right
> thrives on deepening divisions in society – 'us' versus 'them' – while
> the left, when successful, overcomes these cleavages through reforms
> that bridge them. Hence the paradox that earlier waves of reforms
> from the left – Keynesianism, social democracy, the welfare state –
> both saved capitalism from itself and effectively rendered themselves
> superfluous. Absent such a response again, the field will be left wide
> open for populists and far-right groups, who will lead the world – as
> they always have – to deeper division and more frequent conflict.[2]

In practice, the effort to regulate and tame the capitalist economy
which remains the historic purpose of social democracy ought to
mean revisiting the fundamental principle of freedom of movement across Europe: that principle was devised in the 1950s for a

European Community of six members with broadly similar patterns of economic development; in an EU of 28 states with markedly divergent economies, freedom of movement is imposing unsustainable political strains.[3] If this principle were modified while tackling abuses associated with temporary agency and migrant labour in driving down wages and working conditions, at the very least Britain could remain a member of the single market in the aftermath of the Brexit vote, as Vernon Bogdanor has pointed out.

The European political establishment should stop treating freedom of movement as if it is a 'sacred cow': as the world changes and political realities shift, leaders have a duty to reconsider even the most fundamental principles (Tsoukalis, 2016). Moreover, if the left does not address the political and economic dislocation which voters perceive is created by freedom of movement, the demise of European social democracy will be all but guaranteed. As the Dutch deputy prime minister Lodewijk Asscher has suggested:

> We need a new settlement that is fair to the people of both the sending and the receiving countries, and we need to stamp out abuses so that Europe will become and remain a vehicle to improve the lives of its citizens. If we fail to do so we will face a growing decline in support for the European project, which could well mean the beginning of disintegration.[4]

At the same time, centre-left parties have to offer a better compromise between principles and power. The financial crisis has not led to a resurgence of support for the left. Many believed that the collapse of neoliberalism would lead to a renewed faith in social democratic institutions: the active state, Keynesian demand management, social welfare; but it has not come to fruition. Indeed, the left has not succeeded in generating any compelling ideas that offer a decisive step beyond the crisis. The American liberal intellectual Francis Fukuyama has chastised social democratic parties for failing to offer anything distinctive in terms of an alternative conception of how to organise society and the economy, while no longer championing the interests of the struggling middle class.

As the German political scientist Wolfgang Streek (2014) has noted, politics and markets in the advanced democracies are becoming increasingly disconnected. In the 1990s, there was talk of a third way between old style social democracy and the new right, reconciling old conflicts:

- Globalisation meant lower inflation after decades of 'stop-go' policies and industrial militancy;
- Education promised upward social mobility and an end to inequality;
- Economic growth meant investment in public services and the welfare state: at long last, economic efficiency and social justice could be reconciled (Miliband, 2011).

In the wake of the crash and the great recession, the political choices appear to have sharpened markedly:

- Economically, the logic says remain open and embrace international trade; yet the politics says protect what you have and be prepared to go your own way;
- The west needs more economic migrants given long-term demographic change, but politically the demand is for greater controls on the movement of people;
- To ensure future growth and social sustainability, governments should invest in the young; but the most powerful electoral constituency is older voters who want to protect existing entitlements and benefits in the social security system;
- And the world is still confronting the potentially devastating effects of climate change after two centuries of rapid industrialisation and continuing global growth of three per cent per annum (Miliband, 2012; Gamble, 2012; Sapir, 2014).

Social democrats have to develop a governing project in an age when the broad mass of working people, both the traditional blue-collar constituencies and the growing middle class, are facing increasing pressures including an unprecedented compression of incomes and a dramatic living standards squeeze:

- Economic power is shifting from west to east (and often north to south) putting jobs under threat: a process accelerated by the financial crisis;
- The knowledge economy is polarising labour markets leading to a loss of low skilled jobs; the weakening of organised labour makes it ever harder to protect wages;
- The 'resource crunch' has driven up commodity prices and the cost of food and fuel in many developed states;
- Inequality is rising both within and between countries despite the progress of the global south: this is due to the growth of market-based inequalities as well as the decline in the effectiveness of redistribution at the level of the nation state;
- As a result, there is a conundrum facing all centre-left parties: most voters want greater choice and control in their lives, but they also want to be protected from the insecurities generated by globalisation and technological change; they yearn for greater personal freedom; at the same time, they seek security from the adversities of life (Miliband, 2011; Gamble, 2012; Mulgan, 2005).

All of these challenges have to be addressed in a world where faith in politics has been diminishing: political parties are perceived as narrow, unrepresentative cliques ruled by corporate money; there is a lack of compelling ideas and ideological alternatives; the political class is regarded as too remote from citizens; in many societies, politicians appear determined to give power away to the regulators and technocrats. The only way out of this malaise for the left is to engage voters in the bigger choices and trade-offs that our societies face; to resist the 'consumerisation' and marketisation of politics, demonstrating that messy and uncertain as the process might be, politics is still the best hope of improving our societies and making our countries more equal (Stoker, 2006).

POST-BREXIT BRITAIN: EUROPEAN POLITICS
IN A 'POST-TRUTH DEMOCRACY'

The backdrop to this debate about social democracy in Britain is the EU referendum result on 23 June 2016. The decision of British voters by 51.9 per cent to 48.1 per cent to withdraw from the EU was a hammer blow to pro-European social democracy. Many commentators claim they predicted Brexit, but few in the British political class saw it coming: the Bank of England and financial institutions had contingency plans to deal with volatility in the markets; in truth the economic and political establishment (relying heavily on erroneous evidence from the polling industry and the betting markets) believed that remain would creep narrowly over the line. The elites assumed that despite leave being ahead in the final phase of the campaign (having capitalised on heightened fears about intra-EU migration in the event of Turkish membership) the country would turn away from the economic risks entailed in leaving the EU, and would revert unenthusiastically to the status quo. Few commentators foresaw what was happening in regions outside London and the affluent south-east of England, where voters moved in huge numbers towards leave. This is evidence of the growing chasm between the political class and voters, not a propitious sign for British representative democracy.

As to the remain campaign itself, countless postmortems have already been conducted. It was always going to be difficult to win. The case for remain is an argument for the status quo; many voters are dissatisfied with the state of the British economy after a decade of falling living standards and declining real wages. Politics itself has rarely been held in greater disrepute. Anger with a distant and unaccountable bureaucracy in Brussels is fuelled by greater levels of dissatisfaction with Westminster democracy. Nor is there much affection for mainstream politicians in any of the major parties. In this febrile political context where distrust is endemic, any negotiating strategy and future model of UK-EU relations has to acknowledge the democratic will of citizens.

The referendum result is still not easily explained, and we need to understand better why leave prevailed. The conventional narrative is that the leave vote was a revolt by 'left behind' voters who wanted to punish the unruly elites that encouraged policies like untamed freedom of movement, harsh austerity measures, and the disruptive impact of globalisation. Inevitably, the story is more complex. For one, culture was equally, if not more important than economics according to Eric Kaufmann of Birkbeck College, London: the referendum exposed a 'values divide' in Britain as much as a traditional class divide. Research for the British Election Study (BES) by Kaufmann indicates that commitment to authoritarian values is a far stronger predictor of supporting withdrawal from the EU than income or social class: regardless of whether you are rich or poor, if you are in favour of restoring the death penalty, for example, you were more likely to support leave on 23 June.[5]

Nor is post-2008 austerity a sufficiently robust explanation for the remain rout. Some disadvantaged areas of the UK made significantly worse off by cuts in welfare and public services nonetheless voted to remain. Where economic discontent drove voters to reject the EU, the cause was liberalisation programmes enacted 40 years ago alongside the reaction to structural economic change rather than austerity in 2008, as Will Davies has suggested. English towns once dominated by heavy industry and former Welsh mining villages rejected EU membership because both the single market and national government have ostensibly done little to provide them with a viable economic future after decades of deindustrialisation.[6] Of course, both UK governments and EU structural funds have sought to redistribute resources to ailing regions, but as Davies indicates, one of the critical lessons of the referendum campaign is that voters do not want to be dependent on a market liberal state dominated by financial interests in London. These voters want to gain greater capacity to control the destiny of their communities in accordance with working-class traditions of civic pride, emancipation and 'self-help'.

For all of these reasons, making the case to stay in the EU was always going to be tough. Nonetheless, the remain campaign hardly made its task easier. The strategists who shaped its message were well versed in fighting UK general election campaigns in which parties need to secure barely 35 per cent of the popular vote to gain a parliamentary majority, but in a referendum campaign every vote counts. A narrow and cautious appeal to the median voter centred on economic risk and a plea to stay in the EU from big business will not build a sufficiently broad coalition in a tight race. Remain needed to demonstrate that by remaining an EU member we could build an inclusive economy in which globalisation would work for the majority, spreading growth throughout the United Kingdom, where necessary by constructively tackling the excesses of financial capitalism.

Rather than making the referendum a verdict on an out of touch political elite and a failing EU, remain needed to frame the contest as a choice about what kind of Britain we want to be. The remain camp dominated by David Cameron's advisers would never have acceded to such a strategy since rather than confronting head-on the issue of British sovereignty, they sought to avoid it - a catastrophic error that enabled the leave camp to peddle the seductive but illusory myth of 'taking back control'. In truth, Britain is never going to be subsumed into a federal superstate without the explicit agreement of its citizens. National sovereignty is positive rather than negative sum: by pooling sovereignty and resources at the EU level, national governments gain greater room for manoeuvre and are better able to tame the forces of global capitalism. And the fundamental freedom to make choices about the size of the British state, levels of taxation and regulation, the sustainability of the market economy, have been preserved alongside EU membership. All of these arguments tragically fell by the wayside during the campaign.

This still begs the central post-Brexit question: what is to be done? As Andrew Gamble reflects, the set of choices confronting the political class on UK-EU relations hardly looks palatable. The 'Norway-plus' option is the most attractive to the political and financial elite (and indeed to many voters), but unfettered single market access requires acceptance of free movement, budgetary contributions, and EU regulations without an ability to influence the rules of the political game at European level. On the other hand, any shift towards a unilaterialist trade position will inflict an enormous shock on the British economy, dividing the Conservative party from its core support in corporate business and the City of London.[7] Politicians will have to make these decisions within an increasingly dysfunctional and crisis prone political system where the territorial politics of Scottish independence, turmoil in Northern Ireland, and fragmentation in England (witness the attempt by London to secure greater autonomy over taxes and spending) threaten to break the UK apart. As Gamble attests, since the crown in parliament remains the fundamental source of political authority, MPs currently in the House of Commons will have to implement a referendum decision two-thirds of them fundamentally disagree with.

For parties of the centre left, the choices are scarcely more appealing. The danger for British Labour is that it tries to fudge its position given the dilemma the party faces between maintaining the support of predominantly liberal remain voters in metropolitan enclaves, as against appealing to leave supporters in the 'heartland' areas of former industrial England and Wales, alongside more affluent towns in the south and Midlands. Indeed, if Labour were to win the next general election, it would have to gain a substantial number of seats that leaned heavily towards leave in the referendum campaign.[8] The EU referendum has entrenched a new dividing line in British politics between an 'open' and a 'closed' society that threatens to destroy the established party system. What will save the centre left now, however, is not merely adept political positioning but hard-edged, credible policy strategies that lead to action, building bridges between communities at ease with economic change, and those who resent openness:

• First, by developing a new industrial policy that provides a viable growth model for the whole of the UK rather than hoarding wealth in southern England. The state has a role in ensuring a competitive, modernised private sector. All options should be on the table including acquiring public stakes in growth companies, strategic investment in growing sectors notably the green economy, regional assistance and investment programmes, and social ownership of public infrastructure including the railways where economic circumstances allow. Equally essential is following through on political devolution, equipping towns outside urban areas with the tools to rebuild their economic base, not least by developing local and regional production chains.

- Second, national government has to fashion a new compact to deal with globalisation, rebuilding a comprehensive social insurance architecture centred on the principle of contribution for those in work, and security for those who cannot work. The principle of insurance will have to be fundamentally rethought given the changing nature of work.
- Third, more support through public funding has to be provided to areas disproportionately affected by rapid migration flows. The Labour government's Migration Impact Fund was mistakenly cut in the wake of austerity; it needs to be re-established, particularly to invest in social and physical infrastructure throughout hard-pressed areas.
- Fourth, migration across Europe ought to be better controlled by working to create greater stability on the periphery of the EU through a new Marshall Plan for north Africa, concerted action to defend democratic values in Ukraine and the Balkan neighbourhood, alongside robust controls on the EU external border. As already noted, reforms of the fundamental principle of freedom of movement in the EU are also required.
- Fifth, we have to devise effective integration policies that work, focused on language learning for all migrant and refugee entrants to the UK alongside employment and education programmes.

This policy framework, of course, requires comprehensive public funding; it is true that part of the task is to invest existing public sector budgets more effectively. But all of these policies will require sustained investment, and the UK's fiscal position is likely to become more precarious in the aftermath of Brexit: the OECD is currently forecasting that UK GDP will be 3.3 per cent smaller by 2020. One of the lessons of the 2008 financial crisis is that business and the private sector has to do more to support the public policy infrastructure needed to sustain economic openness. The Brexit outcome makes that task even more urgent.

In the past, there has been too much freeriding by corporate business in Britain, yet the referendum result clearly demonstrates the catastrophic consequences of divergence between business and society. The two must be brought back together; the private sector has to contribute more towards the cost of essential public goods. If the UK economy does go into recession having suffered successive structural shocks in the wake of Brexit, Britain will require an immediate stimulus programme: the key will be to support growth and employment not through short-term 'pump-priming' or debt-fuelled consumption, but investing in the pillars of politically and economically sustainable growth that ensure as far as possible, the UK can remain open to the rest of the world.

SUMMARY

For left-of-centre parties, the core political strategy is as it was throughout the 20th century: forging an effective alliance between the middle class, the blue-collar working class, and those in greatest need: the jobless, the economically excluded, the most disadvantaged. In Britain, the great Labour victories of 1945, 1964 and 1997 were achieved by constructing a political coalition between the 'haves' and the 'have-nots', centered on tackling insecurity through the collective institutions of the welfare state, eliminating material inequalities in order to create opportunity throughout society.

Social democrats face tough times ahead, but the centre left must not be unduly pessimistic. If the left and centre left seeks to win elections by bemoaning the state of contemporary society and hankering after a vanishing 'golden age,' it will lose and deserve to do so. Politically, winning elections has become tougher for social democratic parties as a direct consequence of reforms enacted by the left since 1945. Citizens' aspirations are higher; they no longer seek to be alleviated from basic material deprivation; class structures are more complex; voters want choice and they want to be able to influence bureaucracies and politics. These are changes that the left should welcome, even if they make constructing stable political coalitions a harder task. Social democracy has to be upbeat and optimistic about the future.

Social democrats throughout Europe have the opportunity to cultivate new ideas, new governing strategies, and new political narratives; beyond the policies of national governments, economies and societies are increasingly being organised around values of sharing, cooperation and mutuality which are natural territory for the left and centre left. Conservatism is hardly in great shape either: parties of the right were enthusiastic adopters of neoliberal policies, but market liberalism has attacked the very institutions and traditions that conservatism once nurtured. Social democrats again have the chance to dominate the debate intellectually and politically, to shift the centre of gravity in politics towards the left.

The idea of reforming the balance of power in society is a great progressive mission, breaking down power-hoarding public and private monopolies while promoting genuine competition, giving people greater control over their lives in relation to markets and capital as well as the state. It involves the commitment to a 'positive' conception of liberty: the role of public intervention and the state is not merely to remove the barriers to unfettered free enterprise and wealth creation, but to invest positively in the social and economic potential of every citizen while eliminating egregious material inequalities. Moreover, this is consistent with the story of human freedom, social justice, and equal opportunity which has been at the core of social democracy since the late nineteenth century. The third way sought to draw a line under the past; it claimed to be comprehensively different to anything that had gone before. This was counterproductive. Instead centre-left parties need to learn intelligently from their past, especially their reformist fore-bears throughout the generations, including Eduard Bernstein, Jean Jaurès, Willy Brandt, Anthony Crosland, and Olof Palme. Left of centre parties will not regain the political initiative by resorting to technocracy and managerialism. By engaging with this past and by renovating ideas and ideological principles, social democrats can forge a new path to the future.

NOTES

1. J. M. Keynes quoted in G. Shuster, *Christianity and Human Relations in Industry*, p.109, 1951.
2. https://www.project-syndicate.org/commentary/anti-globalization-backlash-from-right-by-dani-rodrik-2016–07.
3. V. Bogdanor, 'If EU leaders listen, there could still be a second referendum', *The Guardian*, 19th July 2016.
4. http://www.policy-network.net/pno_detail.aspx?ID=4504&title=-Stopping-Europes-race-to-the-bottom-Free-movement-precarious-jobs-and-the-populist-signal-
5. http://www.fabians.org.uk/brexit-voters-not-the-left-behind
6. http://www.perc.org.uk/project_posts/thoughts-on-the-sociology-of-brexit
7. http://mei.qmul.ac.uk/news-and-opinion/blog/items/177955.html
8. https://www.buzzfeed.com/chrisapplegate/why-a-pro-eu-party-could-be-screwed-in-the-next-election?utm_term=.fmxXJ45aL#.ekv6oLg4y

BIBLIOGRAPHY

P. Aghion, 'The Smart State', in P. Diamond, T. Dolphin & R. Liddle, *Progressive Capitalism in Britain: Pillars for a New Political Economy,* London: Policy Network, 2014.

M. Albrow, *The Global Age: State and Society Beyond Modernity,* Cambridge: Polity Press, 1996.

J. Andersson, *The Library and the Workshop: Social Democracy and Capitalism in the Knowledge Age*, Stanford: Stanford University Press, 2009.

R. & S. Burgess, 'Can School League Tables Help Parents Choose Schools?', *Fiscal Studies*, Volume 32 (2), pp. 245–278, 2011.

B. Bell & S. Machin, 'Labour market slack in the UK', *National Institute Economic Review*, 229: F4–F11, 2014.

S. Berman, *The Primacy of Politics*, Cambridge: Cambridge University Press, 2006.

M. Bevir & R. Rhodes, *Governance Stories*, London: Routledge, 2005.

M. Blyth, *Austerity: The History of a Dangerous Idea*, Oxford: Oxford University Press, 2011.

J. Callaghan, *The Retreat of Social Democracy*, Manchester: Manchester University Press, 2009.

W. Carlin, 'A Progressive Economic Strategy', London: Policy Network, 2013.

B. Clift & J. Tomlinson, 'Credible Keynesianism? New Labour Macro-Economic Policy and the Political Economy of Coarse Tuning', *British Journal of Political Science*, Volume 37 (1), pp. 47–69, 2007.

J. Cronin, G. Ross & J. Schoch, *What's Left of the Left?* New York: Duke University Press, 2010.

C. Crouch, *The Strange Non-Death of Neo-Liberalism*, Cambridge: Polity, 2011.

J. Curtice, A. Heath & R. Jowell, *The Rise of New Labour*, Oxford: Oxford University Press, 2005.

J.C., 'The new working class', The Economist website, 16 June 2014.

J. Dearden et al., 'Inter-generational mobility in Britain', Research Paper, London School of Economics, 2009.

G. Esping-Andersen, *Incomplete Revolution: Adapting Welfare States to Women's New Roles*, Cambridge: Polity Press, 2009.

G. Esping-Andersen, *Social Foundations of Post-Industrial Economies*, Oxford: Oxford University Press, 1999.

M. Ferrera, *The Boundaries of Welfare: European Integration and the New Spatial Politics of Social Protection*, Oxford: Oxford University Press, 2005.

M. Freeden, *The New Liberalism: An Ideology of Social Reform*, Oxford: Oxford University Press, 1978.

C.B. Frey & M.A. Osbourne, 'The Future of Employment: How susceptible are jobs to computerisation?', University of Oxford Martin School Programme, 16th September 2013.

A. Gamble, *Crisis Without End?,* Basingstoke: Palgrave Macmillan, 2012.

A. Gamble, 'The Future of Social Democracy', Social Europe website, 11 January 2010.

A. Gamble, 'Social Justice in a Shrinking World', in O. Cramme & P. Diamond, *Social Justice in a Global Age*, Cambridge: Polity, 2009.

M. Glasman, 'England, My England!', Prospect, October 2010.

M. Goos & A. Manning, 'Explaining Job Polarization: Routine-Biased Technological Change and Offshoring', London School of Economics Research Paper, 2014.

B. Guy-Peters, 'Back to the Centre? Rebuilding the State', *The Political Quarterly,* Volume 75 (2), 2004.

T. Horton & J. Gregory, *The Solidarity Society: Fighting Poverty and Inequality in an Age of Affluence 1909–2009*, London: The Fabian Society, 2009.

G. Irvin, *Super-Rich: The Rise of Inequality in Britain and the United States*, Cambridge: Polity Press, 2014.

J. Jenson & D. Saint-Martin, 'New Routes to Social Cohesion? Citizenship and the Social Investment State', *Canadian Journal of Sociology/Cahiers canadiens de sociologie*, Volume 28 (1), pp. 77–99, 2003.

A. Lavelle, *The Death of Social Democracy: Political Consequences in the 21st Century*, Aldershot: Ashgate, 2008.

D. Lepianka, W. Van Oorschot & J. Gelissen, 'Popular Explanations of Poverty: A Critical Discussion of Empirical Research', *Journal of Social Policy*, Volume 3 (38), pp. 421–438, 2009.

R. Liddle & F. Lerais, 'Europe's Social Reality', Bureau of European Economic Advisers (BEPA), Brussels: European Commission, 2006.

N. Lowles & A. Painter, 'Fear and Hope: The New Politics of Identity', London: Searchlight, 2011.

J.E. Meade, *Liberty, Equality, and Efficiency*, New York: NYU Press, 1993.

D. Miliband, 'Why is the European Left Losing Elections?', Political Quarterly Lecture, London School of Economics, 8th March 2011.

D. Miller, *Principles of Social Justice*, Cambridge, Mass: Harvard University Press, 1994.

G. Moschonas, 'Electoral Dynamics and Social Democratic Identity: Socialism and its changing constituencies in France, Great Britain, Sweden and Denmark', What's Left of the Left: Liberalism and Social Democracy in a Globalised World, A Working Conference, Centre for European Studies, Harvard University, May 9–10th, 2008.

G. Mulgan, 'Anti-Politics', *The Guardian*, 7th May 2005.

S. Padgett, *A History of Social Democracy in Post-War Europe*, London: Longman, 2003.

C. Pierson, *Hard Choices: Social Democracy in the Twenty-First Century*, Cambridge: Polity Press, 2001.

D. Rodrik, 'Why Do More Open Economies Have Bigger Governments', *The Journal of Political Economy*, Volume 106 (5), pp. 997–1032, 1998.

D. Runciman, *The Confidence Trap: A History of Democracy in Crisis from the First World War to the Present*, Princeton, NJ: Princeton University Press, 2013.

J. Rutherford, 'Labour's Good Society', Social Europe website, 28th October 2010.

M. Ryner, 'An Obituary for the Third Way: The Financial Crisis and Social Democracy in Europe', *The Political Quarterly*, Volume 81 (4), pp. 554–565, 2010.

D. Sage et al., *The Social Reality of Europe After the Crisis*, London: Rowman & Littlefield, 2015.

A. Sapir, 'Still the Right Agenda for Europe? The Sapir Report Ten Years On', *Journal of Common Market Studies,* Volume 52, pp. 57–73, 2014.

D. Sassoon, *One Hundred Years of Socialism*, London: IB Tauris, 1996.

M. Savage & F. Devine, *Rethinking Class: Cultures, Identities & Lifestyles,* London: Penguin, 2015.

A. Sorenson, *Globalisation,* London: Sage, 2004.

G. Stoker, *Why Politics Matters,* Basingstoke: Palgrave Macmillan, 2006.

S. Strange, *The Retreat of the State,* Cambridge: Cambridge University Press, 1996.

W. Streek, 'How Will Capitalism End?', *New Left Review,* Volume 87 (3), May–June 2014.

P. Taylor-Gooby (ed.), *New Paradigms in Public Policy,* Oxford: Oxford University Press, 2013.

L. Tsoukalis, *In Defence of Europe: Can the European Project Be Saved?,* Oxford: Oxford University Press, 2016.

M. Weir, 'The Collapse of Bill Clinton's Third Way', in S. White (ed.), *The Third Way? The Progressive Future,* Basingstoke: Palgrave Macmillan, 1999.

S. White (ed.), *The Third Way? The Progressive Future,* Basingstoke: Palgrave Macmillan, 1999.

R. Wilkinson & K. Pickett, *The Spirit Level: Why More Equal Societies Almost Always Do Better,* London: Allen Lane, 2009.

A. Wren, *The Political Economy of the Service Transition,* Oxford: Oxford University Press, 2013.